THE ATLAS OF
FOOD

Second Edition

Erik Millstone and Tim Lang

First published by Earthscan in 2003
This second edition published 2008

A catalogue record for this book is available from the British Library

ISBN: 978-1-84407-499-0

Produced for Earthscan by
Myriad Editions
59 Lansdowne Place
Brighton, BN3 1FL, UK
www.MyriadEditions.com

Edited and coordinated by Jannet King and Candida Lacey
Designed by Isabelle Lewis and Corinne Pearlman
Maps and graphics created by Isabelle Lewis

Printed on paper produced from sustainable sources.
Printed and bound in Hong Kong through Lion Production
under the supervision of Bob Cassels, The Hanway Press, London

For a full list of publications please contact:

Earthscan Ltd
Dunstan House
14a St Cross Street
London EC1N 8XA
UK
Tel: +44 (0)20 7841 1930
Fax: +44 (0)20 7242 1474
Email: earthinfo@earthscan.co.uk
Web: www.earthscan.co.uk

Earthscan publishes in association with
the International Institute for Environment and Development

Erik Millstone is Professor of Science Policy at the University of Sussex, UK. He has been working on food-related issues since the mid-1970s and is the author of *Food Additives; Additives: A Guide for Everyone; Our Genetic Future; Lead and Public Health* and *BSE: Risk, Science and Governance*, as well as numerous journal and magazine articles on the politics of food and health. He is currently working on a project concerned with reconciling improved food production for poor farmers in developing countries with environmental sustainability, as part of the STEPs centre.

Tim Lang is Professor of Food Policy at City University's Centre for Food Policy in London. He studies how policy affects the shape of the food supply chain, what people eat, and the societal, health, and environmental outcomes. He is a Fellow of the Faculty of Public Health, a Vice-President of the Chartered Institute of Environmental Health and a regular consultant to the World Health Organization and other governmental and non-governmental public bodies. Since 2006, he has been Land Use and Natural Resources Commissioner on the UK Government's Sustainable Development Commission. He is co-author of *Food Wars* and *The Unmanageable Consumer*, and is widely credited as coining the term "food miles".

"Invaluable...I would not be without
the complete set on my own shelves."
Times Educational Supplement

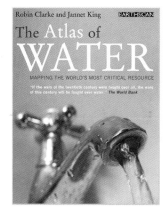

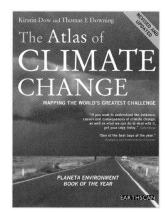

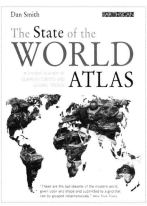

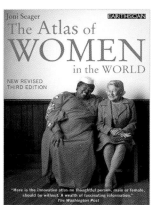

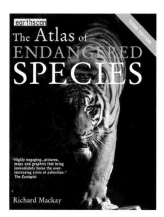

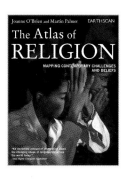

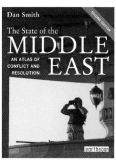

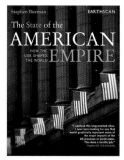

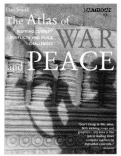

"No-one wishing to keep a grip on the reality of the world should be without
these books." *International Herald Tribune*

"Fascinating and invaluable." *The Independent*

"A new kind of visual journalism" *New Scientist*

Contents

Contributors

The authors would like to thank the following people for their contributions on specific topics:

Lukasz Aleksandrowicz (University of Guelph) *8 Contamination*

Steven Allender and Mike Rayner (Department of Public Health, University of Oxford) *7 Over-Nutrition*

Peter Backman (Horizons FS Limited) *36 Eating Out*

David Barling (Centre for Food Policy, City University, London*) 21 Agricultural Biodiversity*

Simone Baroke (Centre for Food Policy, City University, London) *33 Retail Power*

Paul Brassley (University of Plymouth) *9 Mechanization*

David Buffin (Centre for Food Policy, City University, London) *15 Pesticides*

Charlie Clutterbuck (Environmental Practice@Work) *16 Fertilizers; 23 Greenhouse Gases; 40 Citizens Bite Back*

Alizon Draper and Veronica Tuffrey (Centre for Public Health Nutrition, School of Integrated Health, University of Westminster, London*) 6 Nutritional Deficiencies; 30 Staple Foods; 31 Changing Diets*

Axel Drescher and Johanna Jacobi (University of Freiburg, Germany) *19 Urban Farming*

David Goodyear (Fairtrade Foundation, London) *29 Fair Trade*

Jannet King (Myriad Editions) *1 Current Concerns; 4 Environmental Challenges; 5 Water Pressure; 12 Animal Diseases; 17 Working the Land; 20 Fishing and Aquaculture; 22 Organic Farming; 29 Fair Trade; 37 Fast Food; 34 Organic Food; 40 Citizens Bite Back*

Tim Lobstein (SPRU – Science and Technology Policy Research, University of Sussex) *39 Advertising*

Becky Price (GeneWatch) *13 Agricultural R&D; 14 Genetically Modified Crops*

Geof Rayner (Centre for Food Policy, City University, London) *38 Alcohol*

Peter Stevenson (Compassion in World Farming) *10 Industrial Livestock Production; 25 Live Animal Transport*

Introduction

Investigating what we eat, where we eat and how we eat reveals a remarkable world of contrasting food and drink cultures, represented graphically in this atlas. As you look through it, we hope that a narrative emerges that links the patterns and analyses in each section. For all the people who have contributed to this project, the modern world of food is not a random series of "facts" and "events", but a complex and ever-changing web of industrial, technological, economic, social and political factors that shape the journey food takes from its production on the farm to the eventual consumers. This is reflected in the structure of the book: Part 1 outlines a set of contemporary challenges that confront us, highlighting problematic features of the food system. Part 2 investigates farming, including its numerous inputs, such as machinery, fossil fuels and agrochemicals. Part 3 focuses on international trade in food, and the imbalance it creates between farmers in wealthy countries and those in poorer ones. Part 4 looks downstream, at food processing, retailing, consumption and consumers.

Power in the food chain

Most observers agree that food traders and retailers are the main power brokers in the modern food system. Not always; in some countries, power still lies with land-owners. But generally, it is traders and retailers who control the supply chains, determining not just prices but quality. Despite the rhetoric that the system is driven by individual consumer choices, it is in fact large corporations that make the key decisions, often influenced by what happens in local and global markets, on the commodity and futures trading floors, in banks, factories and laboratories. These decisions can have a huge impact on farmers, who are often dependent on industrial firms to provide them with, for example, seeds, fertilizers, pesticides, machinery and fuel.

The kinds of food that are produced, and the methods used to produce them, are increasingly influenced by others along the chain – but especially by processors and retailers. In reply, corporations often claim they merely respond to consumer demand; otherwise they would be out of business. Consumers are portrayed as the arbiters of choice and taste – and it is true that no-one forces food into our mouths – but when compared with corporations and wider forces, individuals often do feel relatively powerless. Why would we, the world's consumers, choose to starve or to be obese, or suffer from diet-related disease? And most consumers would prefer a food system that did not damage the environment. Poor, hungry people have fewer options than affluent consumers, but even the affluent can only choose from what the food industry has deemed it most profitable to provide.

International food trade is dominated by a handful of exceptionally large corporations. They gate-keep the large quantities of food traded across borders; yet chronic hunger often occurs in countries exporting food. While economists stress the importance of developing countries earning foreign currency from exports, there is no nutritional logic to transferring food from areas where under-consumption is a serious problem to countries and regions characterized by over-consumption; what logic there is, is strictly economic and political.

An unsustainable system

The systematic picture this atlas offers is not meant to imply that the world of food is organized like a well-oiled machine. On the contrary, it is, as always, in a state of flux. Some of its features even point to instability, in the sense that they cannot survive unchanged in the long-term, or even the medium-term, for ecological, economic, social or political reasons. The world would not be able to sustain itself if every country produced and ate food as people do in Europe or the USA. In the UK, for example, people eat food as though the country had around six times its land and sea space. For all to eat in this way would use more land and energy than is available on Earth.

Scientists and technologists have been studying crops, livestock, farming systems and food processing since the 18th century. The rate of technological change in farming and the food systems has been particularly rapid, and changes in the pattern of investment in research, development and innovation have had substantial economic, social and environmental consequences. There is now widespread agreement that natural resources such as land, water and energy are under stress around the world as a consequence of the way the food system operates. Forest clearance has diminished the extent to which natural vegetation has been available to absorb increasing emissions of carbon dioxide, and the cattle farmed on cleared forest land are notorious producers of methane, which is 21 times more potent as a greenhouse gas than carbon dioxide. Through such interactions, the technological, industrial, economic, environmental, social and political aspects of the food system mutually influence each other. These dynamics and interactions not only undermine the sustainability of the food system, they will spark change – whether positive or dire remains to be seen.

High-technology industrial food systems are spreading across the world, raising critical policy questions of strategy, direction, acceptability and sustainability. For example, developing countries ask why it is necessary and acceptable for governments of industrialized countries to subsidize their farmers, while those same governments, and institutions they influence such as the World Bank, insist that the governments of developing countries must *not* subsidize their farmers. From the point of view of poor countries, current policies mean that the livelihoods of developing-country farmers are undermined by cheap imports from industrialized countries, while those industrialized countries operate barriers to the importation of many agricultural products from developing countries. Food-policy issues concerning subsidies and trade rules are not just narrow technical considerations; they are critically important to the reasons why chronic hunger continues to afflict so many poor people in poor countries.

Volatility in the price of agricultural products can be problematic, especially if it is accompanied by volatilities in supplies. Significant food surpluses can result in sharp price reductions, which may adversely affect farm incomes and decisions about future investments, and in turn lead to price rises and discontent amongst consumers, especially in the urban areas. One of the main reasons why the governments of the industrialized countries tentatively began to accept responsibility for managing agricultural markets between the First and Second World Wars, and more firmly after 1945, was to try to manage buffer stocks to stabilize prices and supplies. More recently, and especially after the creation of the World Trade Organization in 1994, and the liberalization and globalization of agricultural markets, official interventions have diminished, and most food commodity prices continued to fall as they had for years. But in 2006 and 2007, food prices began to rise – world grain prices in particular. This was probably due to a combination of factors – including rapid growth in demand from China, more volatile temperatures, less reliable rainfall, more extreme events, probably linked to climate change, plus a mix of speculation and funds looking for stable investments. The policy decision by the USA and EU to support biofuels to replace oil was a trigger. As oil prices rose towards $100 a barrel, the demand for plant-based fuel sources grew, especially for heavily subsidized corn-based crops in the North American prairies. That, in turn, has added to crop scarcities and to rising prices. This new agricultural policy mix raises critical questions with which we all, not just politicians, need to engage. Old questions about supply management or land use jostle alongside new ones about genetic modification and biofuels as to where solutions lie.

Increasing complexity of food chains

The atlas shows that food-supply chains cannot be represented as simple, straight lines. Food often follows a circuitous route before someone eats it. A large proportion of the agricultural crops produced in the industrialized countries are not consumed directly by people, but indirectly as meat, milk and dairy products, with vast quantities of grain and beans grown only to be used as animal fodder. This may be economically efficient, but it is nutritionally and ecologically *in*efficient.

As the interconnections and loops of the food-supply chain have become increasingly complex, the distance between producers and consumers has widened – both literally and metaphorically. One effect has been growing consumer concern and mistrust. The strong, if relatively short-lived, public rejection of beef in the UK in 1996, when it was officially acknowledged that BSE-contaminated meat was responsible for the degenerative brain condition vCJD, underlined how vulnerable industrialized farming is to volatile public opinion and to undetected pathogenic contamination. Food companies recognize this, which is one reason why they spend vast sums on advertising and sponsorship – to try to create trust based on brand loyalty. Advertising failed to persuade European consumers to accept the introduction of genetically modified foods or the cultivation of GM crops; in practice and ironically it undermined public confidence in GM foods. Problems of trust in official regulatory regimes, and in the products of the food industry, have not yet been solved. Protecting brand integrity and trust has also become a driver of corporate behaviour. If public opinion changes, or adverse scientific findings emerge, brands can become vulnerable.

One particularly tangible consequence of the increasing complexity of the food chain and distances between producers and consumers is the enduring problem of microbiological food poisoning, which continues to afflict poor and rich communities alike. As food chains have lengthened the opportunities for pathogens to spread have increased too. Barriers to the transfer of contamination have been undermined by the astonishing speed and distance travelled by both food and people – which was fuelled by cheap oil. Oil is no longer cheap, yet the food economy is locked into oil-based technologies. Without plentiful oil, irrigation, agro-chemicals, shipping, flying and trucking foods over long distances becomes increasingly expensive. There are active debates concerning the environmental significance of transporting food and agricultural products, but few pretend that current practices are acceptable or that current trends are sustainable.

Hunger, poverty and food justice
The irony is that enough food is produced on this planet to feed everyone adequately, *if* it were to be shared uniformly. Some over-eat while others are malnourished. Technologically, the problems of food production has been solved, but political, economic and social forces result in severely skewed patterns of production, distribution and consumption. The world lacks food justice.

Technological change can create problems as well as solutions. Particular caution is needed when transferring technology from one society to another, especially from a wealthy country to a poor country. Crop varieties and production methods that require relatively high-priced industrial inputs (fertilizers, pesticides, irrigation and machinery) tend to benefit wealthy, and especially highly subsidized, farmers but disadvantage poorer farmers who are unable to make the necessary investments. While technological change may result in more food being produced in aggregate, it may increase the number of hungry farmers by amplifying the inequalities between rich and poor. A change to less labour-intensive agricultural practices can have a devastating effect in areas where the vast majority of people are, or were, employed on the land.

We now live in a world in which chronic under-nutrition coexists with a growing population suffering from chronic over-nutrition. Under- and over-nutrition can be seen as opposite sides of the same coin. Resources devoted to improving the nutritional well-being of poor and hungry people have diminished as resources devoted to increasing the quantity, availability and choice of foods to people who are already over-eating have increased. Since the 1990s, the incidence of obesity has risen in numerous countries at alarming rates, and many of their governments are urgently trying to devise effective policy responses, preferably without upsetting their voters or corporate friends. Often the motive is the sheer cost of diet-related ill health to healthcare systems.

Our approach in this atlas

This atlas therefore seeks to provide not only the evidence with which to describe the global food system, but also a framework within which to make sense of the ways in which it has developed and will evolve. It tries to do justice to the current predicament, highlighting important trends and offering an analysis of the underlying dynamics. It also poses the questions: how can it be improved? Where lies progress?

The direction in which forces are operating is not just one-way, nor is it pre-determined. Powerful institutions and organizations can be rather vulnerable. The distribution of power is frequently challenged and may be changeable. Worldwide, a movement of informed groups and alliances has emerged, questioning current practices, demanding changes, making connections. This constellation of actions, campaigns and organizations is providing a powerful progressive voice in food policy. Even when small in comparison to big corporations or governments, they can influence beyond their numerical weight. The Fairtrade movement, for example, is attempting to redress the balance in favour of the small producer, while other international movements represent the interests of the environment, labourers and consumers against existing power blocs.

The focus of these organizations varies, but includes providing information, campaigning on specific issues, championing causes and implementing alternatives. Some push the "inside track" of policy; others try to shift the centre of gravity in policy, or reframe policy agendas. Certainly, in this century, there is wider recognition that the *status quo* is not an option. One example is the increase in certified local suppliers (many of whom are organic farmers). The importance of urban farming also demonstrates, not just that some short food chains persist, but that there is a growing demand for shorter food chains, less processing, and a far more direct, traceable relationship between producer and consumer.

Wherever you stand or eat in the modern food system, we hope you find the atlas as stimulating as the writing team has found it to produce.

Erik Millstone

SPRU – Science and Technology Policy Research,
University of Sussex

Tim Lang

Centre for Food Policy,
City University, London
March 2008

PART 1 Contemporary Challenges

The current global agricultural and food system has many structural defects. Despite centuries of productivity and efficiency increases, a chronic problem of malnutrition continues to afflict a large proportion of poor people, especially those in developing countries. This situation persists despite the fact that, in aggregate, there is enough food to feed everyone a sufficient diet. Undernutrition, characterized by too few calories and/or too few nutrients, is fundamentally linked to poverty, lack of income and entitlement or rights.

Although recent years saw reductions in farm-gate prices, to the detriment of farmers around the world, since early 2007 there have been substantial increases in food prices. This has been caused by a combination of factors. High oil prices impact on food production and transport costs, and have encouraged the drive towards the cultivation of crops for biofuels. This in turn has reduced the amount of grain available for food, which has led to an increase in grain prices and increasingly urgent warnings of diminishing global food stocks. Of course, the people most affected by rising prices are poor people everywhere, given that they are likely to spend the highest proportion of their incomes on food.

The practices of farmers, traders, food processors and retailers make heavy demands on the environment, increasing the rate at which resources such as rainforest, soil and water are depleted, and the rate of pollution from fossil fuels and agri-chemicals. Once again, the adverse consequences of these unsustainable practices fall disproportionately on the poor, and especially on those in the poorest countries.

It would be a mistake, however, to suppose that problems of food-related public and environmental health are confined to the impoverished. Bacteria, viruses and chemical contaminants are found everywhere, and diet-related problems such as obesity and diabetes are becoming increasingly prevalent in rich countries, and among well-off citizens of countries where poorer people are dying of malnutrition.

The levels of waste, pollution and soil degradation, and the use of energy and water in food and agriculture could be markedly reduced. Social and technological changes could help slow or reverse some forms of land degradation, and diminish the adverse environmental and health impacts of the food system. International co-operation is essential, however, to reduce greenhouse gas emissions, and to make our food systems more ecologically, socially and economically sustainable.

CURRENT CONCERNS

100 million
tonnes of cereals were diverted for biofuels in 2007

FOOD PRICES AROUND THE WORLD – both local and imported products – rose by nearly 40 percent in 2007, caused by a combination of factors that include the financial markets, environmental conditions, and policy decisions.

Booming Asian economies are leading to a heightened demand for all kinds of food, but in particular for meat and dairy products, which rely on an increased supply of grain for animal feed. Cereal stocks in 2007/08, especially those of wheat, are predicted to be at their lowest since the early 1980s.

Extreme weather conditions, including both droughts and floods, have affected both local food supplies and prices, and the global grain trade.

High oil prices mean higher transport costs, which clearly impacts on global trade, but also on local retail prices.

The increased demand for biofuels – in part a response to the need to combat climate change – is also a contributing factor, since it reduces the amount of grain available for food. Campaigners in Africa are highlighting a worrying trend towards the purchase of large areas of land by commercial companies intent on growing crops for fuel.

While higher food prices may have little impact on some sectors of society, for people who may need to spend as much as 70 percent of their income on food, they bring real hardship, and even starvation. Protests against the high cost of staple foods took place around the globe in 2007, and in some countries government action was taken to freeze prices.

Early in 2008, the World Food Programme warned that the sharp increase in the price of cereals was affecting its capacity to provide food aid for some of the world's most vulnerable people.

DECLINING GLOBAL CEREAL STOCKS
2005–08
million tonnes

- 473 — 2005–06
- 427 — 2006–07
- 405 — 2007–08

USA – maize for biofuels

In the USA, the use of maize for ethanol production more than doubled between 2000 and 2006. In 2007, 20% of the maize crop was used to produce ethanol, estimated to rise to 25% in 2008.

Mexico – food riots

In January 2007, thousands of people protested against a doubling in the price of tortillas caused by farmers in the USA and Mexico replacing edible maize crops with industrial maize for processing into biofuels.

Peru – bread price

The price of imported wheat increased by 50% during 2007, resulting in rising bread prices.

Bee colony collapse

The recent collapse of honey bee colonies in Europe and the Americas may impact on agricultural production. Bees pollinate over 90 food crops, and play a role in one in three mouthfuls in the average American diet.

Russia – food price freeze

In October 2007, the Russian government persuaded food producers and retail chains to freeze the price of some staple foods for an agreed period to try and avoid unrest in the run-up to national elections.

Kazakhstan – export ban

Early in 2008, the government warned that it would be limiting grain exports.

Kyrgyzstan – bread price

The price of bread in the capital increased by 50% in 2007, while salaries and pensions increased by only 10%.

China – biofuel crop ban

In June 2007, China banned production of ethanol from food crops.

China – dairy demand

The increasing demand for milk and dairy products in China has led to it not only being the third-largest milk-producing country but the largest importer of milk products.

Mauritania – rising food prices

In November 2007, people protested at rising food prices. The price of locally grown foods had increased by 28%, and imported wheat by 75%.

Yemen – food riots

In August and September 2007, people protested in Yemen about rising food prices, caused by higher import prices.

China – big freeze

Early in 2008, the most severe winter weather in 50 years killed millions of livestock and damaged crops, leading to soaring food prices.

Ghana and Benin – biofuel crops

Plans are being made to plant millions of hectares with jatropha and sugar cane to produce biofuels.

Bangladesh – cyclone

In 2007, a cyclone destroyed a rice crop worth $600 million and the price of rice rose by 70%.

Australia – drought

The long-running drought affecting much of Australia led to a halving of the wheat harvest in 2007, and to no grain being exported from east-coast ports.

Zambezi valley – floods

Substantial flooding early in 2008 will have a devastating effect on agriculture in the region.

Tanzania – biofuel crops

Thousands of small-scale farmers have been evicted to make way for jatropha and sugar plantations.

INCREASING COST OF FOOD IMPORTS
2006–07
US$ trillion

2006

2007

$512 trillion

$429 trillion

developed countries

$234 trillion

$186 trillion

developing countries

17

UNDER-NOURISHED PEOPLE

Distribution by economic status of country
2003 or latest available data

industrialized
9 million

transition
25 million

developing
820 million

Total: 854 million

MORE THAN ENOUGH FOOD is produced to feed everyone in the world, and yet more than 850 million people do not get enough food to lead active and healthy lives. They are consuming too little protein and energy to sustain a healthy weight, and suffer from deficiencies in the composition of their diet that leave them vulnerable to disease. In 2005, the UN FAO estimated that the world's total production of cereals was about 2.2 billion tonnes. Divided equally between the 6.5 billion people in the world, that would give each person approximately 340 kilograms of cereal a year – sufficient to provide at least 2,000 calories of energy a day for everyone.

Most undernourished people live in countries where food is in chronically short supply because of war, natural disasters, poor food distribution, low productivity, or a number of these factors combined. What they all have in common is that they are poor. In wealthy countries, by contrast, the amount of food available is sufficient for people to be able to consume significantly more than the 2,500 calories recommended by nutritionists, even though the food they eat may result in the other extreme of poor nutrition – obesity.

Country averages hide wide disparities. In the fast-growing economies of Brazil, China, and India, the more prosperous citizens are switching to western-style diets, high in animal fats and sugars, while their poorest compatriots spend an ever-higher proportion of their household income on food, and still suffer from undernutrition.

The World Food Programme and other agencies aim to supply the most vulnerable people with basic foodstuffs, responding both to long-term needs and to emergency situations as they arise.

CANADA

USA

A child die of hunger every

5

seconds

BAHAMAS
MEXICO
CUBA
JAMAICA HAITI DOMINICAN REP.
BELIZE
GUATEMALA HONDURAS ST KITTS & NEVIS ─── ANTIGUA & BARBUDA
EL SALVADOR ─── DOMINICA
NICARAGUA ST VINCENT & ─── ST LUCIA
GRENADINES ─── BARBADOS
COSTA RICA ─── TRINIDAD & TOBAGO
PANAMA VENEZUELA
GUYANA
COLOMBIA SURINAME

ECUADOR

PERU

BRAZIL

BOLIVIA

CHILE PARAGUAY

ARGENTINA
URUGUAY

Bolivia

Severe floods in 2007 and 2008 left thousands of families in need of WFP assistance.

THE COST OF FOOD

Expenditure on food as a percentage of household expenditure on consumable goods
2004 or latest available data

USA	UK	Pakistan
14%	22%	48%

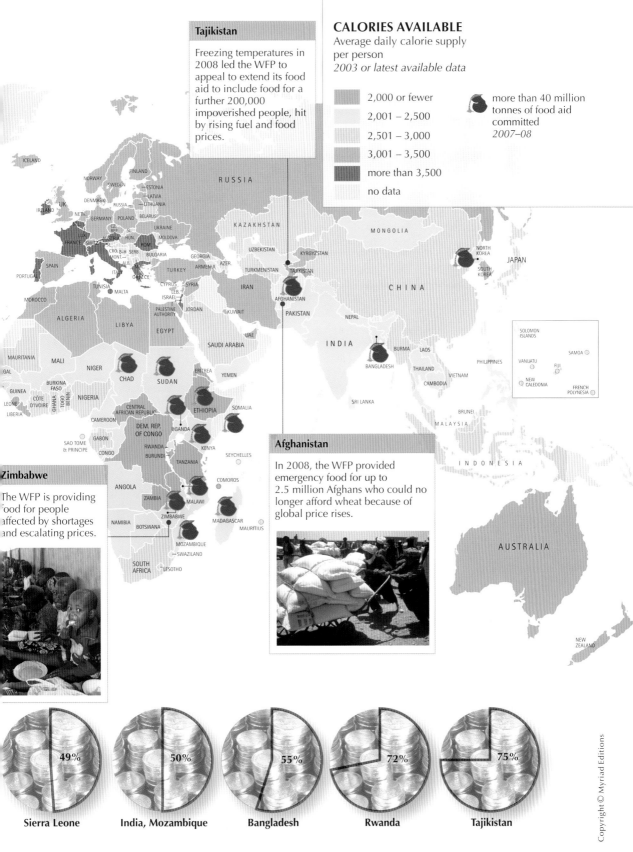

Tajikistan

Freezing temperatures in 2008 led the WFP to appeal to extend its food aid to include food for a further 200,000 impoverished people, hit by rising fuel and food prices.

CALORIES AVAILABLE

Average daily calorie supply per person
2003 or latest available data

- 2,000 or fewer
- 2,001 – 2,500
- 2,501 – 3,000
- 3,001 – 3,500
- more than 3,500
- no data

more than 40 million tonnes of food aid committed
2007–08

Afghanistan

In 2008, the WFP provided emergency food for up to 2.5 million Afghans who could no longer afford wheat because of global price rises.

Zimbabwe

The WFP is providing food for people affected by shortages and escalating prices.

49% Sierra Leone

50% India, Mozambique

55% Bangladesh

72% Rwanda

75% Tajikistan

**Kilogrammes
of cereal
produced
per hectare
in 2005:**

UK

7,229

Niger

394

CHRONIC UNDER-NUTRITION is not a consequence of overall scarcity, but of unequal access to land, technology, education and employment opportunities, coupled with a whole range of socio-economic and environmental factors. The world's population is unevenly distributed, as is the quantity of food produced, and there is a mismatch between the largest populations and the most productive agricultural land and farming methods.

Although the overall production of cereals has grown roughly in line with population increase, the regions where the largest strides have been made in terms of agricultural production are not those that have experienced the greatest increases in population. Productivity has improved substantially in South America and Asia in the last half century, but in Sub-Saharan Africa, where the need is greatest, the increase was not as marked, and in some parts productivity has declined. Climate change is likely to affect agriculture in many and

complex ways, but current predictions show reduced outputs in South Asia and Sub-Saharan Africa.

Food is redistributed around the globe both a trade and aid – and a mixture of both – but th redistribution is neither sufficient to solve th problem of under-nutrition nor desirable as long-term solution. Improvements are neede in agricultural practices and in social structure so that more food can be produced an consumed where it is most needed. Whil technological change can raise agricultura productivity, if the technologies are to expensive for poor farmers they will make th well-off richer and the poor even poore Technological change without social chang can therefore aggravate inequalities.

Predictions for further population growth vary, but even if the rate of increase continue to slow, as it has done since 1970, the numbe of people in the world is still likely to excee 9 billion by 2050, with more than 60 percent c people living in cities.

POPULATION AND PRODUCTIVITY

▬▬▬ number of people (billions) *1960–2005*

■ ■ ■ number of people (billions) *projected to 2050*

▬▬▬ total cereal produced (billion tonnes) *1965–2005*

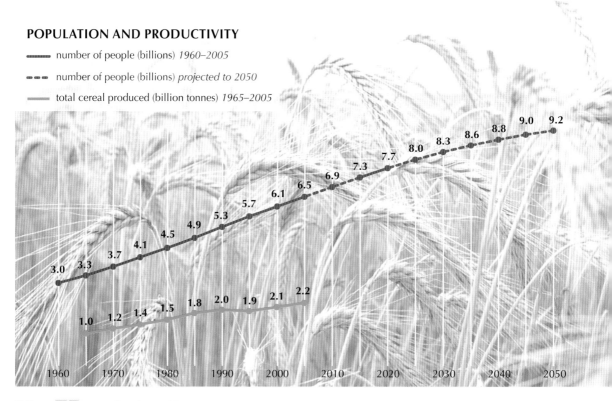

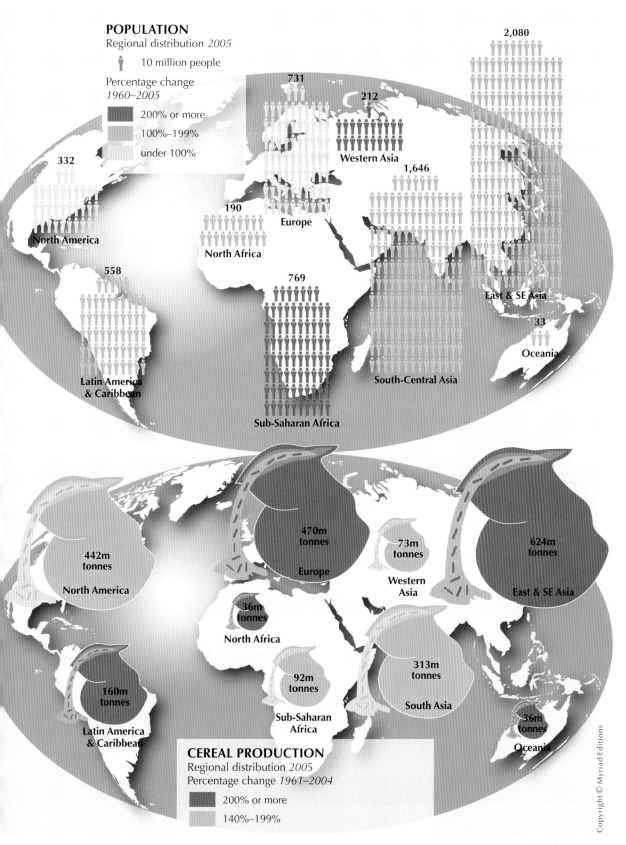

POPULATION

Regional distribution *2005*

10 million people

Percentage change
1960–2005

200% or more

100%–199%

under 100%

332
North America

558
Latin America
& Caribbean

731

212
Western Asia

190
North Africa

Europe

769
Sub-Saharan Africa

1,646
South-Central Asia

2,080

East & SE Asia

33
Oceania

442m
tonnes
North America

160m
tonnes
Latin America
& Caribbean

470m
tonnes
Europe

36m
tonnes
North Africa

92m
tonnes
Sub-Saharan
Africa

73m
tonnes
Western
Asia

313m
tonnes
South Asia

624m
tonnes
East & SE Asia

36m
tonnes
Oceania

CEREAL PRODUCTION

Regional distribution *2005*
Percentage change *1961–2004*

200% or more

140%–199%

4 ENVIRONMENTAL CHALLENGES

SOIL DEGRADATION
1981–2003

land where productivity has declined

12%

AGRICULTURAL PRODUCTIVITY has increased over the past 50 years, but the adverse environmental impacts of those changes have often not been included in commercial prices and so have been mostly tolerated or ignored. It is now clear that the pollution, soil degradation, and loss of habitat and biodiversity caused by current methods of food production and transport are going to make it difficult for current levels of productivity to be maintained or improved on in the future. In an attempt to reduce carbon-dioxide emissions, crops are being grown for biofuels, to substitute for fossil fuels. This is proving ecologically counter-productive, however, and is diminishing the amount of food produced worldwide.

Soil degradation caused by wind or water erosion, nutrient depletion, chemical pollution or salinization is a problem in all regions of the world, with an assessment in 1990 concluding that a quarter of the soil used for growing crops or grazing livestock showed signs of degradation. Ongoing research using satellite imagery to assess changes in productivity

indicates that productivity declined o 12 percent of all land between 1981 and 2003 The study of soils and their degradation i increasingly being recognized as a key issue i the context of food production, and of climat change, with an evaluation of the work of th Food and Agriculture Organization concluding in 2007, that conservation of lands and soil should be given greater priority.

There is considerable scope for reducing waste, pollution and soil degradation, as well a the use of energy and water in the food chain Social and technological changes could enabl many of those problems to be addressed, wit some forms of land degradation reversed, an the rate of progression of others slowec International co-operation is essential, howeve to reduce greenhouse gas emissions, make foo production systems more ecologically an economically sustainable, and to exten educational and economic opportunities to poc people in developing countries, to allow then to adapt and to develop sustainably.

RAINFOREST LOSS
1990–2005

square kilometres lost

area lost as percentage of total rainforest in region

Deforestation

The increasing demand for agricultural land is contributing to the destruction of rainforests around the globe. While tropical timber is the immediate product of this deforestation, around two-thirds of the cleared land is subsequently used for pasture, and a third for arable farming,

much of it managed by large companies responding to an increase in meat and dairy consumption worldwide, and a growing market in soybean and oil palm products.

While attention has been turned to losses in the Amazon and Congo forests, Indonesia

has lost a quarter of its forest, and the Philippines a third.

Because the soils in rainforests are generally shallow and low in nutrients, they are susceptible to erosion, which quickly leaves the land unsuitable for agriculture and leads to further deforestation.

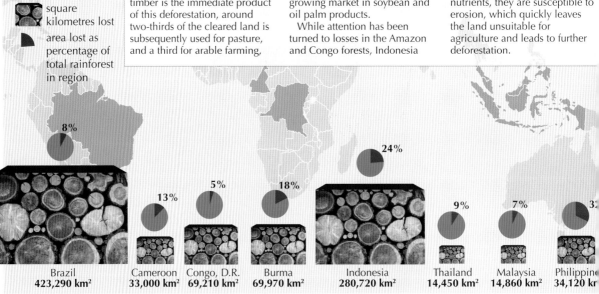

Brazil	Cameroon	Congo, D.R.	Burma	Indonesia	Thailand	Malaysia	Philippine
8%	13%	5%	18%	24%	9%	7%	3%
423,290 km²	33,000 km²	69,210 km²	69,970 km²	280,720 km²	14,450 km²	14,860 km²	34,120 kr

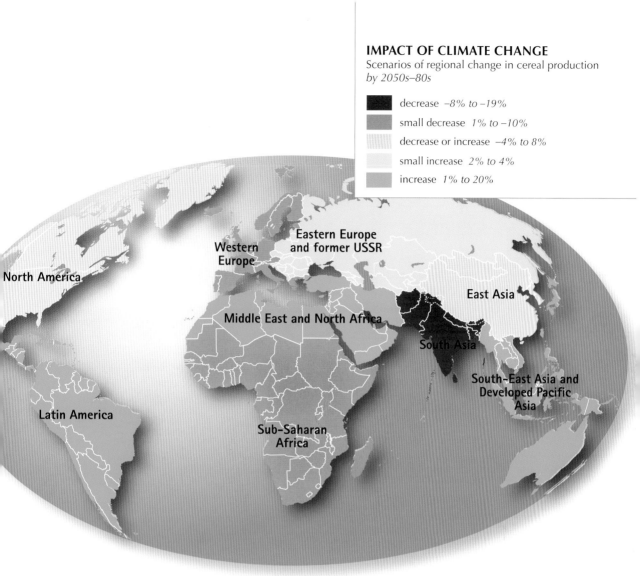

IMPACT OF CLIMATE CHANGE
Scenarios of regional change in cereal production
by 2050s–80s

- decrease *−8% to −19%*
- small decrease *1% to −10%*
- decrease or increase *−4% to 8%*
- small increase *2% to 4%*
- increase *1% to 20%*

North America

Western Europe

Eastern Europe and former USSR

East Asia

Middle East and North Africa

South Asia

South-East Asia and Developed Pacific Asia

Latin America

Sub-Saharan Africa

Predicting the impact of climate change on food production is difficult because so many factors are involved. It is reasonable to assume that a rise in sea-level, already occurring as a result of thermal expansion, will affect low-lying cropland in countries such as Bangladesh, either by inundating it, or by leading to the intrusion of saltwater into underground aquifers, making the land too saline for agriculture, and reducing the availability of fresh water for irrigation or drinking.

Weather patterns are becoming increasingly unpredictable. Intense tropical storms at unseasonable times damage crops and increase food insecurity, as do prolonged droughts.

Agriculture is adaptable, however. Crops can be planted and harvested at different times, and new varieties developed that are more tolerant of stress than those now in use. In Asia, where there is little room for expansion of the agricultural area, global warming may actually enable farmers to move higher up mountain slopes and to more northerly latitudes.

But even if, with a changing climate, the total quantity of food produced remained stable by increasing production in some regions, it is probable that productivity in other regions, including South Asia, and Sub-Saharan Africa, will decline, making hundreds of millions of people increasingly dependent on imported food, with serious political, economic and social consequences.

Proportion of food emergencies caused by flood or drought in 2002:

80%

Proportion of freshwater withdrawals used by agriculture:

70%

MANY COUNTRIES already have insufficient fresh water. An increase in population will see many more experiencing water scarcity or water stress by 2050, while climate change will also undoubtedly have an impact on water supplies.

A country's average water supply obscures much regional variation. California's burgeoning urban population is putting an increasing strain on the state's limited resources, and in China the wheat-growing north is more water-stressed than its largely rice-growing south. Some countries, such as Egypt, are heavily dependent on water flowing in from another country, increasing their vulnerability.

Irrigated crops are crucial to food security, and since 1950 the area under irrigation has doubled. Some methods are very wasteful of water, however, and badly drained irrigation can also lead to increased salinity. But support for farmers to enable them to develop small-scale, low-tech irrigation systems is vital to improving food security in poorer regions.

Some countries are able to compensate for a scarcity of water by importing food. In China, much river water in the north is diverted from the fields to more profitable industrial uses, generating currency to pay for imported wheat to offset any shortfall. However, this makes China dependent on the global wheat market, and increases its food insecurity. Many less industrialized countries, especially those in Africa, are much more vulnerable to water stress: when they experience drought they are too poor to buy food elsewhere.

Although the effects of climate change on water supplies are difficult to predict with precision, it is possible that the Middle East, Central Asia and southern Europe, already experiencing water stress, will see decreased river flows by the end of this century. Elsewhere, increased temperatures may initially increase glacial melt water flows from mountain ranges, but ultimately the flow may dry up, leading to devastating water shortages in areas such as northeast India, Bangladesh, and China – some of the most intensively farmed areas of the world.

Amount of water needed to produce daily food for one person: up to

5,000 litres

IRRIGATED LAND
As percentage
of arable land
2003

Sub-Saharan Africa 4%

Oceania 5%

Europe 8%

South America 9%

North America 10%

Central America & Caribbean 19%

Middle East & North Africa 30%

Asia 34%

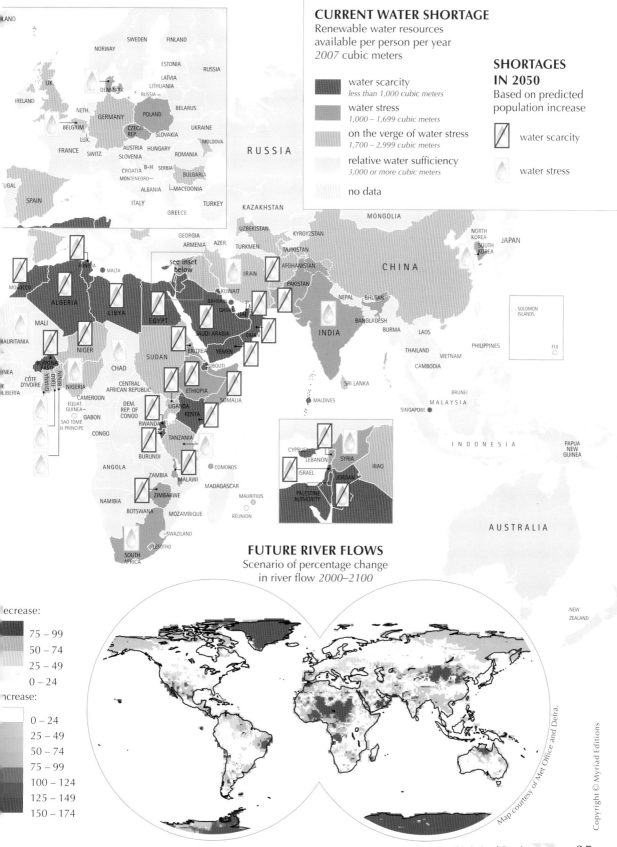

CURRENT WATER SHORTAGE
Renewable water resources
available per person per year
2007 cubic meters

water scarcity
less than 1,000 cubic meters

water stress
1,000 – 1,699 cubic meters

on the verge of water stress
1,700 – 2,999 cubic meters

relative water sufficiency
3,000 or more cubic meters

no data

SHORTAGES IN 2050
Based on predicted
population increase

water scarcity

water stress

FUTURE RIVER FLOWS
Scenario of percentage change
in river flow *2000–2100*

Decrease:
- 75 – 99
- 50 – 74
- 25 – 49
- 0 – 24

Increase:
- 0 – 24
- 25 – 49
- 50 – 74
- 75 – 99
- 100 – 124
- 125 – 149
- 150 – 174

Map courtesy of Met Office and Defra.

11 Animal Feed

up to

500,000

children

**become blind
each year
because of
vitamin A
deficiency**

UNDER-NUTRITION is a major public health problem. It comes in many different forms, and can be caused by an inadequate amount of food, but also by a deficiency of certain nutrients in the diet. Different types of under-nutrition often occur in the same region, and they are almost always associated with poverty.

The overall incidence of all kinds of under-nutrition is much higher in developing than in industrialized countries. The type of under-nutrition caused by a shortage of food is called protein-energy malnutrition, and is often associated with infectious diseases, such as measles and diarrhoea. This combination is a major cause of premature death, especially among children in South Asia and Africa.

Other kinds of under-nutrition, such as iodine deficiency, are caused by a shortage of specific vitamins and minerals in the diet. Again, other factors often contribute to causing these deficiencies, such as infections and intestinal parasites that, for instance, reduce our ability to absorb nutrients from food.

Vitamin A deficiency (VAD) is a major public health problem, affecting 140 million to 250 million pre-school children. It is a leading cause of blindness in developing countries and leaves sufferers at increased risk of infections.

Iron deficiency anemia is the most common kind of micro-nutrient deficiency worldwide, and is also prevalent in industrialized countries.

Some vitamin deficiency syndromes, including rickets (vitamin D deficiency), scurvy (vitamin C deficiency), pellagra (niacin deficiency) and beri-beri (thiamine deficiency), have been largely eradicated through extensive public health programmes, although they sometimes occur when people are dependent on a restricted supply of foods, such as may occur in refugee camps. International public health bodies continue in their efforts to eradicate the remaining micronutrient deficiencies by, for instance, mass supplementation of vitamin A and iodine. However, under-nutrition caused by shortage of food continues to be a huge problem.

up to

250

million

**pre-school children
worldwide
have vitamin A
deficiency**

MEXICO

BELIZE
GUATEMALA HONDURAS
EL SALVADOR NICARAGUA

COSTA RICA
PANAMA

HAITI DOMINICAN REP.

DOMINICA

VENEZUELA

COLOMBIA

ECUADOR

PERU

BRAZIL

BOLIVIA

2

billion

**people
are
anaemic**

Iodine Deficiency Disorders (IDD):
- affect over 740 million people
- are most prevalent in mountainous regions and river plains, where iodine has been leached from the soil by glaciers or floods
- causes goitre (enlarged thyroid gland), mental retardation in children and reduced mental capacity in adults
- are preventable by, for instance, fortifying salt with iodine

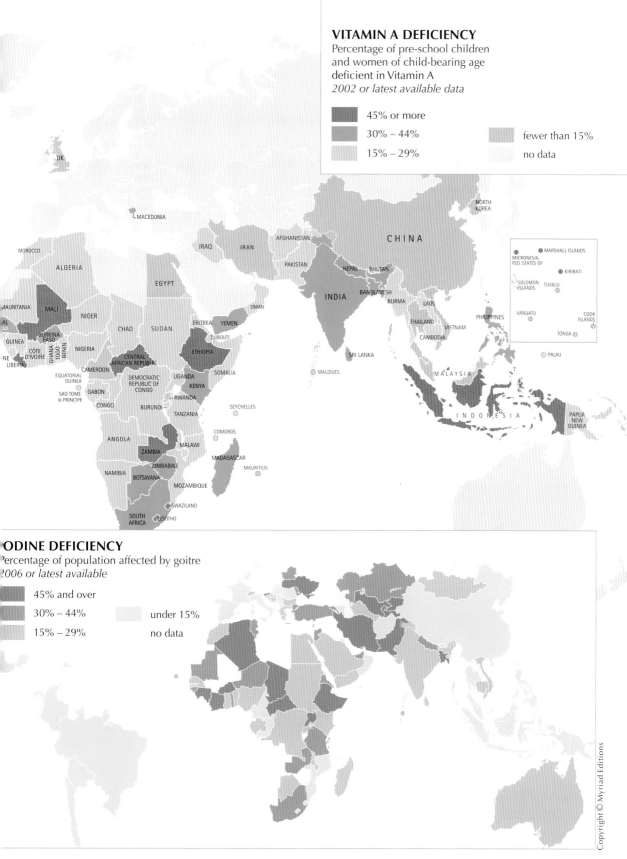

VITAMIN A DEFICIENCY

Percentage of pre-school children
and women of child-bearing age
deficient in Vitamin A
2002 or latest available data

- 45% or more
- 30% – 44%
- 15% – 29%
- fewer than 15%
- no data

IODINE DEFICIENCY

Percentage of population affected by goitre
2006 or latest available

- 45% and over
- 30% – 44%
- 15% – 29%
- under 15%
- no data

Copyright © Myriad Editions

OVER-NUTRITION

OBESITY

Percentage of people considered obese
2005 compared with early 1980s

women 1980s
women 2005
men 1980s
men 2005

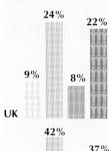

UK

24%

22%

9%

8%

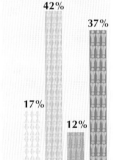

USA

42%

37%

17%

12%

PEOPLE IN INDUSTRIALIZED countries tend to lead sedentary lifestyles and eat more than they need. But the incidence of obesity is increasing worldwide. When countries industrialize, eating habits change and people tend to supplement their traditional diets, high in fruits, vegetables and cereals, with meat and dairy products.

Obesity can lead to diabetes, and this is rapidly becoming a worldwide epidemic. Diabetes is most common in industrialized countries, but recent reports suggest that it is increasing most rapidly in Asia and the Caribbean.

Both diabetes and obesity increase the risk of coronary heart disease (CHD). Until the 1980s CHD was common in industrialized countries, but improvements in medical treatment have led to falling rates in North America, Western Europe and Australia. In Japan, and in countries where people have maintained their traditional, plant-based diets, rates of CHD are low, while in Russia and Eastern Europe, rates are continuing to rise.

In general, premature deaths from CHD are twice as common in men as in women, but in some regions this difference is narrowing. Indeed, diets worldwide are tending to converge, with the growth of fast-food outlets and global trade, and in many developing countries the incidence of heart disease is increasing as a consequence.

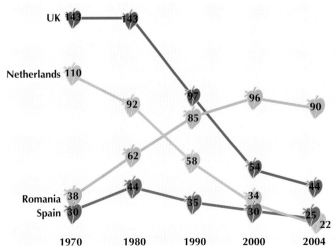

UK 143 — 143

Netherlands 110

92

97

96

90

85

62

58

54

44

Romania 38

44

35

34

25

Spain 30

30

22

1970   1980   1990   2000   2004

CORONARY TRENDS
Number of people aged under 65 dying each year from CHD per 100,000 population
1970–2004

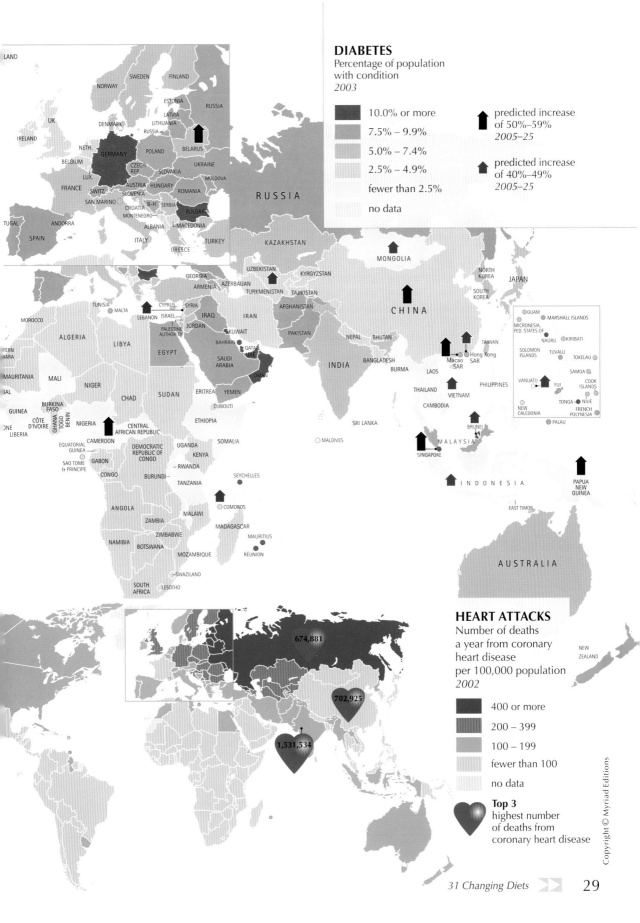

DIABETES

Percentage of population
with condition
2003

- 10.0% or more
- 7.5% – 9.9%
- 5.0% – 7.4%
- 2.5% – 4.9%
- fewer than 2.5%
- no data

predicted increase
of 50%–59%
2005–25

predicted increase
of 40%–49%
2005–25

HEART ATTACKS

Number of deaths
a year from coronary
heart disease
per 100,000 population
2002

- 400 or more
- 200 – 399
- 100 – 199
- fewer than 100
- no data

Top 3
highest number
of deaths from
coronary heart disease

674,881

702,925

1,531,534

8 CONTAMINATION

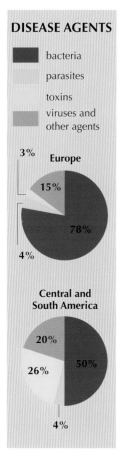

DISEASE AGENTS

- bacteria
- parasites
- toxins
- viruses and other agents

Europe

3%
15%
78%
4%

Central and South America

20%
26%
50%
4%

20%
of child deaths are caused by diarrhoea

AROUND 1.8 MILLION DEATHS a year are caused by diarrhoea, largely contracted from consuming contaminated food or water. Most of the deaths are among children, and almost all are in developing countries, although the problem is increasing in the industrialized world. The globalization of food production and trade, and the popularity of foreign travel, has led to foodborne diseases crossing borders and continents. With more people eating food prepared out of the home, the risk of infection is also increasing.

Over 200 disease agents can be transmitted in food and water. In Europe and the USA, bacteria such as salmonella, associated with industrialized farming, are prevalent. In the tropics, waterborne bacteria and cholera predominate; in coastal areas natural toxins associated with reef fish play an important role. Several new pathogens have recently emerged and others have become resistant to antibiotics.

Although healthy adults in industrialized countries rarely die as a result of contaminated food, the elderly and the very young are more vulnerable. Up to 15 percent of people who survive a serious gastrointestinal illness are left with a chronic condition, including kidney damage and rheumatoid arthritis. In developing countries, foodborne infections, combined with chronic under-nutrition, result in a large number of deaths.

Establishing the true incidence of illness caused by contaminated food and water is difficult because reporting systems are either unreliable or, in many non-industrialized countries, nonexistent. The rates shown on the map are therefore at least partly a reflection of the efficiency of those systems. Even when studies are carried out, figures vary widely, depending on what is actually measured.

What is clear is that illness caused by consuming contaminated food and water is a global problem. Measures needed to combat it include improved public health programmes, more effective water management to increase access to safe water, and improved agricultural practices.

CANADA

USA

MEXICO
BAHAMAS
CAYMAN IS.
CUBA
JAMAICA
PUERTO RICO
BELIZE
VIRGIN IS. (US)
VIRGIN IS. (UK)
GUATEMALA
HONDURAS
MONTSERRAT
DOMINICA
NICARAGUA
MARTINIQUE
BARBADOS
COSTA RICA
TRINIDAD & TOBAGO
PANAMA
VENEZUELA
SURINAME
FRENCH GUIANA
ECUADOR
BRAZIL
PARAGUAY
ARGENTINA
URUGUAY

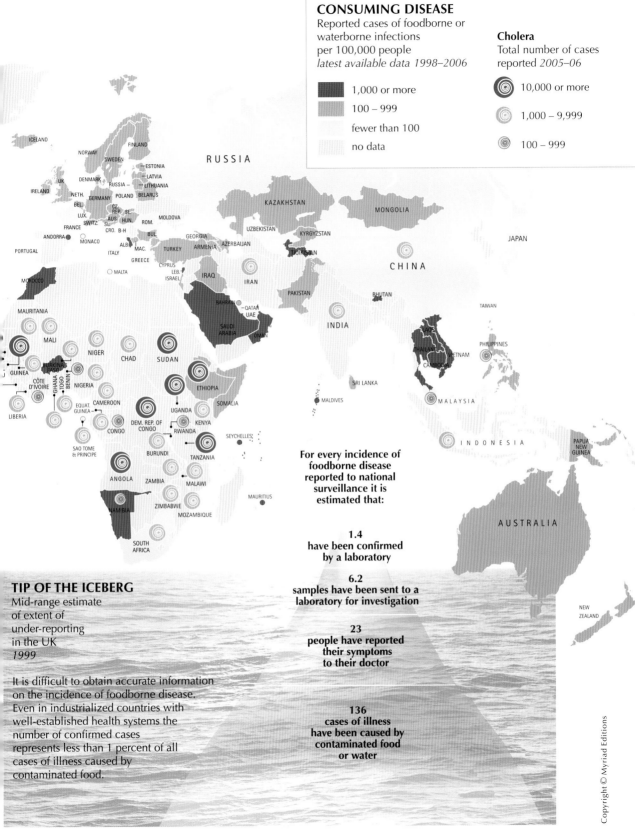

CONSUMING DISEASE

Reported cases of foodborne or waterborne infections per 100,000 people
latest available data 1998–2006

- 1,000 or more
- 100 – 999
- fewer than 100
- no data

Cholera
Total number of cases reported *2005–06*

- 10,000 or more
- 1,000 – 9,999
- 100 – 999

For every incidence of foodborne disease reported to national surveillance it is estimated that:

1.4
have been confirmed by a laboratory

6.2
samples have been sent to a laboratory for investigation

23
people have reported their symptoms to their doctor

136
cases of illness have been caused by contaminated food or water

TIP OF THE ICEBERG

Mid-range estimate of extent of under-reporting in the UK *1999*

It is difficult to obtain accurate information on the incidence of foodborne disease. Even in industrialized countries with well-established health systems the number of confirmed cases represents less than 1 percent of all cases of illness caused by contaminated food.

PART 2 Farming

Agricultural mechanization, and intensive rearing of poultry, cattle, pigs and, more recently, fish have made farming increasingly dependent on industrial inputs such as fertilizers, herbicides, insecticides and fungicides. A large proportion of the world's crops is being fed to animals, so that people who can afford it can consume evermore meat and fish. Not only does intensive livestock farming lead to more frequent animal disease and reliance on antibiotics, with implications for both animal and human health, but it places a strain on the water system, with water shortages in some areas widely predicted to cause a future crisis in food production.

Rapid technological change has been supported by substantial research and development programs, but resources have been largely concentrated on raising the economic efficiency of farming in industrialized countries, while the needs of some of the least productive and poorest farmers receive only a fraction of R&D funding. Biotechnology companies are developing genetically modified crops, promising increased yields that will feed more people in poor countries, and a reduced need for agrochemicals. Their opponents argue that GM crops are at best irrelevant, and at worst harmful, to the poor and the environment.

Although evidence about climate change has been building for decades, its seriousness has only been acknowledged relatively recently, with the 2006 reports of the Intergovernmental Panel on Climate Change serving as rare examples of a fruitful interaction between science and government. The contribution of agriculture to the world's emission of greenhouse gases (GHGs) is a serious challenge, not just to producers but also to consumers. Choices made when purchasing food and drink are one of the most significant ways in which individuals can reduce the GHGs for which they are indirectly responsible.

The manufacture and use of nitrogen fertilizers also make a major contribution to GHGs, but even methods of farming that reject their use probably depend heavily on oil-powered equipment. Tractor-driven tillage is an essential component of organic farming – in industrialized countries at least – replacing the agrochemicals used by intensive systems. Proponents of small-scale farming argue that only labour-intensive systems can start to reduce environmental impacts. Old policy questions return. What is land for? Whose interests should take priority: those of urban or rural people? A new policy agenda is emerging for farming worldwide: how to combine adequate supplies, sustainable methods and health-enhancing output.

9 MECHANIZATION

Ratio of tractors to agricultural workers in Rwanda

1:71,000

THE MECHANIZATION of farming began in the 19th century with the development of the threshing machine, the seed drill and the reaper. But the major breakthrough was the application of the internal combustion engine in the early 20th century. This produced the farm tractor and associated machinery, as well as the combine harvester and machines such as corn dryers, shearers and milking machines.

Since the 1960s, tractors have played an increasing part in agriculture worldwide. They have also become ever more powerful; even though the total number of tractors has changed little since 1990, their total power has increased.

The use of tractors tends to mirror economic developments, with countries in Sub-Saharan Africa, South America and Asia being the least mechanized. In around 40 countries there is not even one tractor between 1,000 agricultural workers and their dependants.

In some countries, mechanization has occurred at a furious rate. These range from African countries such as Nigeria and Burkina Faso, to those in the Middle East, Asia, and eastern Europe. Some terrains, such as the terraced fields of Southeast Asia, are unsuitable for tractors. Yet even in countries such as Indonesia and Thailand there has been a notable increase in their use, although these are relatively small machines, for use on the wet rice fields, and a far cry from the giants of the North American prairies.

The USA, Canada and several European countries have more tractors than people involved in agriculture. However, some of the most technically advanced agriculture in the world is found in the Netherlands and in New Zealand, where the greater importance of animal production means that fewer tractors are required than in primarily arable areas.

INCREASED TRACTOR POWER
Typical tractor horsepower
1920s, 1950s and 2000

2000 240hp

1950s 24hp

1920s 12hp

Brazil – contrasts

While highly mechanized soybean production is taking place in the recently opened up northwest, the northeast of the country is mainly cultivated by small-scale, poor farmers.

TRACTORS
Number of tractors per 1,000 people
in agricultural population
2002

1,000 or more	less than 1
500 – 999	no data
100 – 499	more than 1,000% increase 1965–2002
1 – 99	

INCREASING MECHANIZATION
Number of tractors worldwide
1948–2002

Year	Value
1948–52	6.0
1961	8.0
1966	13.8
1970	15.3
1975	17.9
1980	21.3
1985	24.9
1990	26.7
1995	26.5
1998	26.2
2002	26.7

Copyright © Myriad Editions

35

**Battery hens
in the USA
are given
standing room**
of less than
a sheet of
office paper

INDUSTRIAL LIVESTOCK PRODUCTION is a system of rearing animals using intensive production-line methods that aim to maximize the amount of meat, milk and eggs, while minimizing costs. It has dominated animal agriculture in the European Union (EU) and North America since the 1950s and is becoming increasingly widespread in developing countries.

Industrial livestock production generally inhibits animals from behaving naturally, often causing them pain and serious health problems. In some countries, campaigns against such methods have influenced public opinion and government agencies. The EU has banned battery cages for egg-laying hens from 2012 and sow gestation crates from 2013. However, in the USA, improvements in animal welfare are coming much more slowly.

Intensive farming may also be harmful to human health. Animals in cramped conditions easily catch and transmit diseases, which may then be passed to humans. Farmers routinely using antibiotics on animals may be contributing to antibiotic-resistance among humans, and the use, in some countries, of growth hormones in beef cattle has been linked with human infertility. The practice of injecting dairy cows with hormones to increase milk yields has also raised health concerns for both animals and humans.

The conversion of crops into meat is a nutritionally inefficient and costly way of feeding rapidly increasing populations. Yet countries of Europe and North America are not alone in rearing large numbers of animals for meat. Production is increasing in South America, China, South-East Asia and elsewhere, with farmers adopting industrial methods, often encouraged by foreign investors seeking new markets for equipment, or outlets for crop

PIG-MEAT PRODUCTION
2005
million tonnes

2.0	2.3	2.6	3.1	4.5	9.4	51.2
Denmark	France, Vietnam	Canada	Brazil, Spain	Germany	USA	China

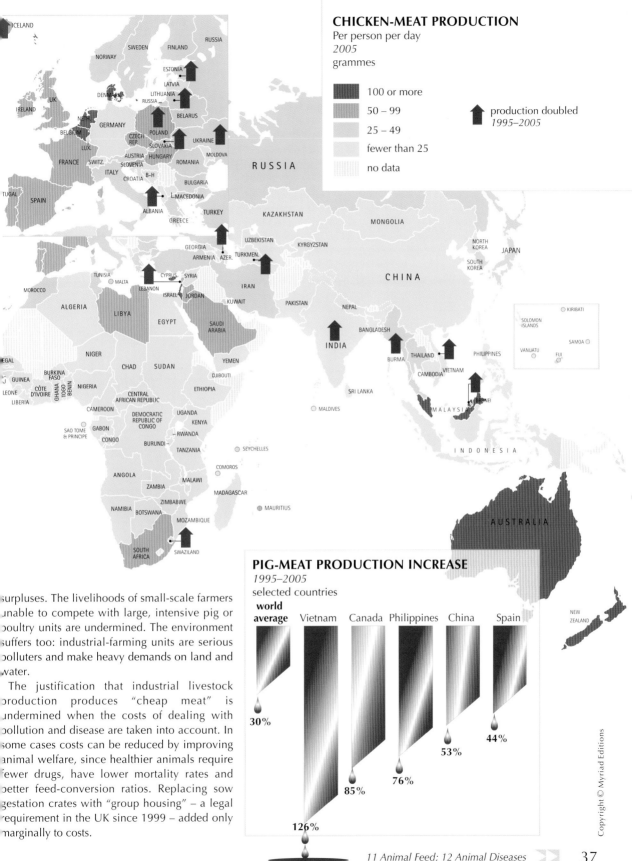

CHICKEN-MEAT PRODUCTION
Per person per day
2005
grammes

- 100 or more
- 50 – 99
- 25 – 49
- fewer than 25
- no data

↑ production doubled
1995–2005

surpluses. The livelihoods of small-scale farmers unable to compete with large, intensive pig or poultry units are undermined. The environment suffers too: industrial-farming units are serious polluters and make heavy demands on land and water.

The justification that industrial livestock production produces "cheap meat" is undermined when the costs of dealing with pollution and disease are taken into account. In some cases costs can be reduced by improving animal welfare, since healthier animals require fewer drugs, have lower mortality rates and better feed-conversion ratios. Replacing sow gestation crates with "group housing" – a legal requirement in the UK since 1999 – added only marginally to costs.

PIG-MEAT PRODUCTION INCREASE
1995–2005
selected countries

world average: 30%
Vietnam: 126%
Canada: 85%
Philippines: 76%
China: 53%
Spain: 44%

Copyright © Myriad Editions

11 ANIMAL FEED

73%
of grain grown
in Canada
is used to feed
livestock

WATER
Used to produce
rice and
grain-fed beef

3,000
litres
water:
1kg
rice

15,000
litres
water:
1kg
beef

10kg
of feed
produces
1kg
of beef

MOST PEOPLE eat mainly vegetarian diets. In affluent countries, however, consumption of meat, eggs, milk and dairy products has steadily increased since the 1950s – a trend that is now evident in China, India and other countries with fast-developing economies.

Technological advances in crop production have generated cheap and plentiful grains and pulses, providing major financial opportunities for livestock farmers. But while livestock farming may make economic sense in the short-run, it makes less nutritional or ecological sense in the long-run. Many more people can be fed from a given area of land if the crops grown are eaten directly by people rather than being fed to animals.

Livestock farmers rearing grain-fed cattle transform relatively cheap maize, soybeans, oats and wheat into relatively expensive meat. In the USA, 400,000 hectares – an area larger than Germany – is used to grow animal feed. Around 80 percent of the world's commercial soybean harvest, and about a third of the world's cereal harvest and commercial fish catches, are consumed by animals, yet much of the nutritional value of the feed is lost in its conversion to meat.

Intensive production of meat, eggs and milk is much more environmentally demanding than traditional forms of arable farming. Livestock production contributes extensively to soil erosion and desertification, with 85 percent of topsoil loss in the USA directly attributable to ranching. In the USA it creates an estimated 1.3 million tonnes of manure a year, some of which runs off and pollutes waterways. Even without factoring in the amount of water used to grow the feed and nurture the livestock, and the energy used to produce the fertilizers needed to grow the feed, it is clear that this pattern of consumption is unsustainable.

Rearing livestock intensively also creates conditions in which veterinary diseases spread rapidly. Feeding maize to cattle adversely affects their digestive system and adds to their stress; these effects are treated with veterinary medicines, including antibiotics, which are often administered to animals not only to cure, but also to try and prevent disease.

66%
of deforestation
in Central and
South America
is to create pasture
for livestock

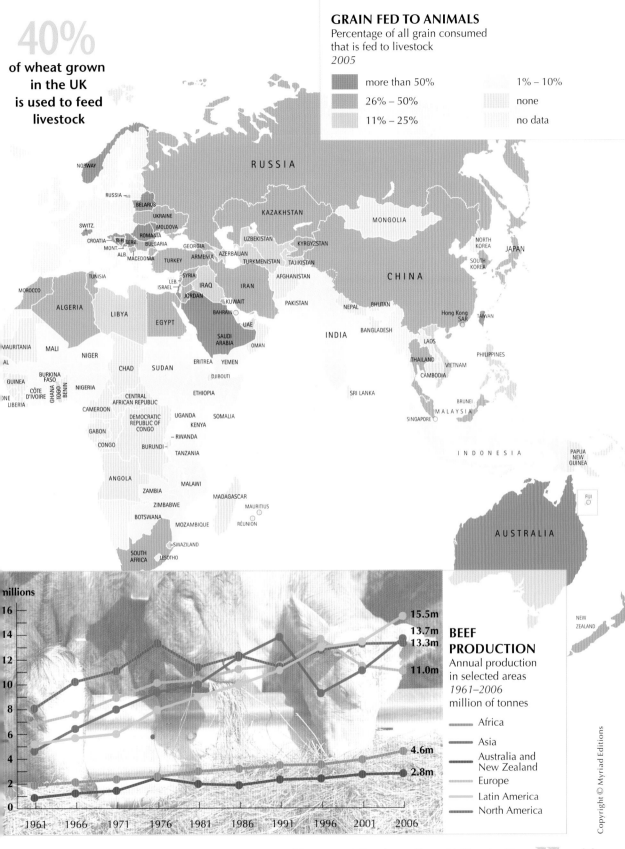

40%
of wheat grown in the UK is used to feed livestock

GRAIN FED TO ANIMALS
Percentage of all grain consumed that is fed to livestock
2005

- more than 50%
- 26% – 50%
- 11% – 25%
- 1% – 10%
- none
- no data

BEEF PRODUCTION
Annual production in selected areas
1961–2006
million of tonnes

- Africa
- Asia
- Australia and New Zealand
- Europe
- Latin America
- North America

15.5m
13.7m
13.3m
11.0m
4.6m
2.8m

millions: 16, 14, 12, 10, 8, 6, 4, 2, 0

1961 1966 1971 1976 1981 1986 1991 1996 2001 2006

**Contagious
bovine
pleuropneumonia
in Africa
causes annual
losses of
up to**

$2
billion

HEALTHY LIVESTOCK provide more meat, eggs and milk than unhealthy livestock. Animal diseases, and the measures taken to control them, can therefore have a major adverse economic effect, ranging from the £3 billion lost in the 2001 UK foot and mouth outbreak, to the hardship and starvation faced by subsistence farmers in poor countries.

Infections can spread very rapidly, especially when animals are intensively housed, slaughtered and processed, or when they are ill-nourished or otherwise stressed. At least 15 animal diseases can, according to the World Organisation for Animal Health, have the potential for "very serious and rapid spread across international borders, with serious socio-economic or public health consequences". People's diets can be affected by a shortage of protein or dairy products following the death of their livestock, and crops may not be harvested if vital draught animals sicken or die.

The outbreaks of avian flu in Vietnam in 2004 and 2005 led to the slaughter of 44 million birds (17 percent of the country's poultry), costing the Vietnamese economy some US$120 million and the poorest Vietnamese households, those most dependent on poultry, an average 7 percent of their income. In Africa, Rift Valley fever causes cows to miscarry, so the farmers lose their calves and obtain less milk. Newcastle disease, which is endemic among domestic fowl in many countries, affects the birds' egg-laying and, at worse, kills them.

In an attempt to control outbreaks of infections in their herds and flocks, farmers in industrialized countries use large quantities of veterinary drugs, especially antibiotics. Industry and government officials claim that veterinary drug-use is safe because it is well-regulated, but critics have long argued that the misuse of veterinary antibiotics can contribute to the development of antibiotic-resistant bacteria in animals and in humans.

8
times
**the amount
of antibiotics
given to
humans
is used on
farm animals
in the USA**

BIRD DISEASES
Confirmed infection
of selected diseases
2005– January 2008

Newcastle disease

• highly pathogenic
avian influenza H5N1

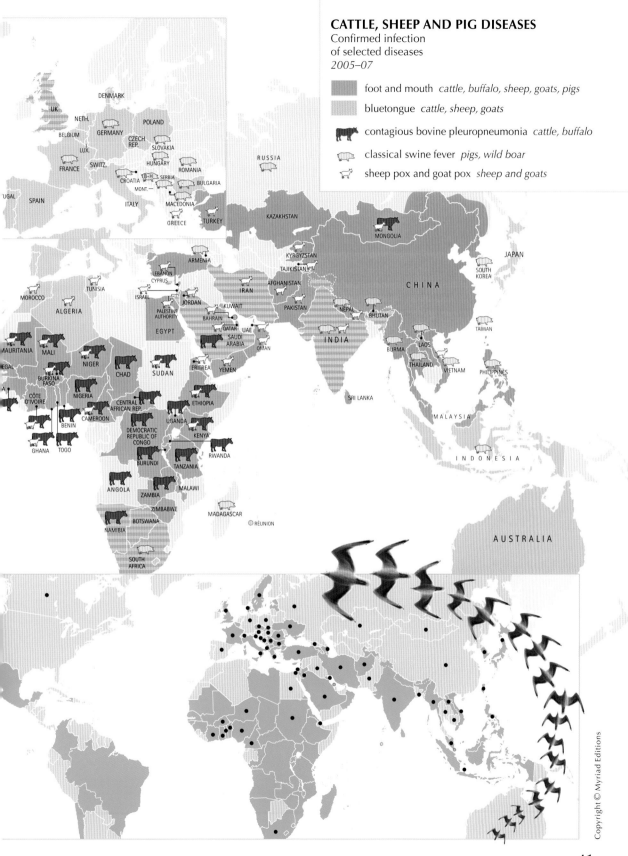

CATTLE, SHEEP AND PIG DISEASES
Confirmed infection
of selected diseases
2005–07

foot and mouth *cattle, buffalo, sheep, goats, pigs*

bluetongue *cattle, sheep, goats*

contagious bovine pleuropneumonia *cattle, buffalo*

classical swine fever *pigs, wild boar*

sheep pox and goat pox *sheep and goats*

Copyright © Myriad Editions

41

UNTIL THE EARLY 1980s, agricultural research and development (R&D) in industrialized countries was largely publicly funded and freely available to farmers. Research was carried out at all levels – from basic science, through to its application on the farm and ways of improving productivity. In recent years, however, local food surpluses, especially in the EU, have meant that priorities have switched to improving the performance of the products after they have left the farm – storing them safely, and enhancing their shelf-life and suitability for processing.

The application of science to agriculture is now seen as the domain of the market-led private sector, with research focusing largely on the needs of capital-intensive farming. The focus of this research is also changing. In the USA, for example, 80 percent of private-sector funding in 1960 was spent on agricultural machinery and on food-processing, whereas funding is now aimed at research into plant breeding and veterinary products.

Over 90 percent of agricultural research in developing countries is funded by public bodies. The financial rewards are often insufficient for private companies, although the development of new strains of rice may attract future private funding. Research has expanded more rapidly in countries in Asia, the Pacific Rim and North Africa than in Sub-Saharan Africa, Latin America and the Caribbean.

The Consultative Group on Internation Agricultural Research (CGIAR) plays a influential role in funding and guiding researc policy for developing countries, supportir 15 international research centres, with ov 8,500 scientists and staff, the majority local recruited, working in over 100 countrie CGIAR is largely dependent on funding fro organizations such as the World Bank – i largest single donor – and from individu industrialized countries. It focuses on usir technology to raise total food production, b there have been complaints from poor farme that the technologies developed by the CGIA institutes are inappropriate for their needs. response, a movement known as Farmer First attempting to base research on farmers' ow perception of their needs, rather than on th ingenuity of experimenting scientists.

Research into plant breeding and farmir technologies tends to be specific to a region climate. Although some technologies suitab for tropical conditions are being developed temperate countries, less than 28 percent of publicly funded R&D is taking place in th tropics, with the needs of some of the lea productive and poorest countries bein neglected. Between 2005 and 2006, CGIAR International Centre for Tropical Agricultu suffered an 8 percent reduction in its operatir budget.

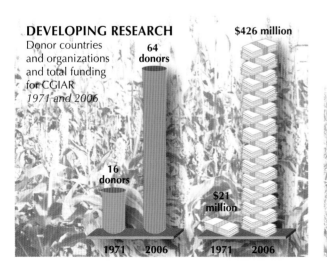

DEVELOPING RESEARCH
Donor countries and organizations and total funding for CGIAR
1971 and 2006

64 donors

$426 million

16 donors

$21 million

1971   2006   1971   2006

PUBLIC–PRIVATE SPLIT
Proportion of funding from public and private organizations
2000
international dollars (2000)

private 8%

public 92%

private 55%

public 45%

Developing countries total: $14.1 billion

Developed countri total: $22.8 billio

GM MARKET GROWTH
Sales of seed of herbicide-tolerant
and insect-resistant plants
1998–2005
US$ billions

- $1.6 — 1998
- $2.4 — 1999
- $2.7 — 2000
- $3.0 — 2001
- $3.3 — 2002
- $3.9 — 2003
- $4.7 — 2004
- $5.3 — 2005

Advantages
- GM crops may increase yields.
- Crops can be modified to grow in dry areas or where salinity is high.
- Levels of nutrients such as betacarotene can be increased in staple crops.
- Vaccines can be cheaply produced in plants.
- Crops are less costly to manage.

Disadvantages
- Research is not primarily aimed at the needs of poor.
- Farmers will become dependent on biotech companies for supplies of expensive GM seeds and other inputs such as branded herbicides.
- GM genes might "escape", and GM crops grow where they are not wanted, and contaminate non-GM crops.
- Crops that are genetically modified to produce pharmaceuticals could accidentally end up in the food chain.

Biotechnology companies are investing heavily in research into GM crops, and they want to ensure that they receive a financial return on their investment by controlling who has access to genes and GM plants. They are doing this in two ways. First, they are claiming patent protection for the genes they use and the GM crops and seeds they produce. This gives them control of the commercial exploitation of their "inventions" for 20 years and allows them to charge royalties or license fees for their use. Farmers growing plants from patented seed will have to pay royalties on any seed they buy or keep for re-sowing, raising their costs and excluding the poorest farmers from using GM seed. Many people have raised objections to this on the grounds that discoveries about nature should not be patentable.

Secondly, the biotechnology companies are exploring Genetic Use Restriction Technology (GURTs), which ensures that farmers using their seed are forced to purchase additional chemicals that need to be applied before the new seeds or plants will function.

Herbicide tolerance and insect resistance remain the focus of research into new GM crops, with these traits being introduced in a wider range of crops. Crops with higher yields, disease resistance, drought tolerance and enhanced nutritional properties are all being researched as a way of dealing with climate change and an increasing population. However, none of these crops is yet being grown on a commercial scale.

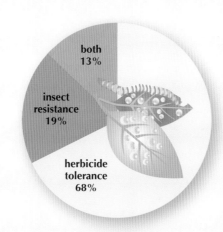

- both 13%
- insect resistance 19%
- herbicide tolerance 68%

GM TRAITS
Type of trait
as percentage of
total GM crops
2006

GM CROPS
Type of crop
as percentage of
total GM crops
2006

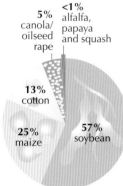

5%
canola/
oilseed
rape

<1%
alfalfa,
papaya
and squash

13%
cotton

25%
maize

57%
soybean

SINCE THE FIRST GM PLANT was produced in 1984 over 170 different crops have been genetically modified and tested in field trials.

Genetic modification allows genes from one species to be moved into another, whereas conventional breeding only involves the same species, or very closely related species, which restricts the gene pool and available characteristics. Most genetic modifications involve genes taken from bacteria, viruses and other plants. Sometimes, genes have been transferred from animals to plants. Fish genes that give tolerance to cold have been moved into strawberries, for example, but these are unlikely to be commercialized because of consumer resistance.

GM crops were first grown commercially in 1996, in the USA, where the area under cultivation has since increased to nearly 55 million hectares. Elsewhere, the increase has been less dramatic, except in Brazil, which only entered the market in 2003 but now has the third-largest area of GM crops.

Consumer resistance has affected the wider adoption of GM crops, with fears expressed about their long-term impact on human health. In some countries it is therefore mandatory to state if GM ingredients have been used on the label. This means that the food and agriculture industry must keep GM and non-GM crops separate. However, as the area of GM crops grown increases this is becoming more difficult. Over one-third of the contamination incidents recorded over the last ten years involved maize – probably because its pollen is able to travel for many miles on the wind.

Resistance to GM crops has also focused on their effect on the environment. Crops tolerant of herbicides allow more efficient weed removal but this may adversely affect species of wildlife that depend on weeds for food. The use of insect-resistant crops may reduce the use of insecticides in some circumstances, but the toxin in the GM crops may harm non-target species and have a damaging effect on the food chain.

GM maize contamination
In 2005, Syngenta's BT10 variety of GM maize was found to have been mixed with another variety, and to have been grown commercially in the USA in 2000–04. This untested GM maize had been shipped throughout the world.

10
CANADA

24
USA

8
MEXICO

GUATEMALA

HONDURAS

NICARAGUA

COLOMBIA

ECUADOR

PERU

7
BRAZIL

BOLIVIA

PARAGUAY

CHILE

ARGENTINA

URUGUAY

GM rice contamination
In 2006, Bayer's LLRICE601, which had been grown in field trials in 2001, was found throughc the rice-growing are of the USA, and in food and feed supplies around the world.

GM CROPS WORLDWIDE
Area under cultivation
1996–2006
hectares

1.7m
1996

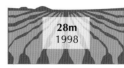

28m
1998

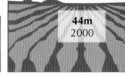

44m
2000

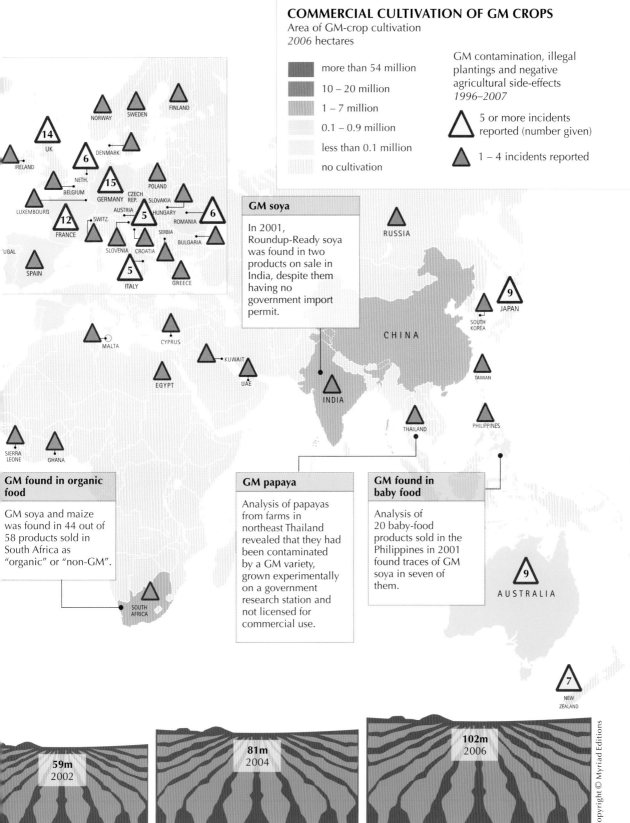

COMMERCIAL CULTIVATION OF GM CROPS

Area of GM-crop cultivation
2006 hectares

- more than 54 million
- 10 – 20 million
- 1 – 7 million
- 0.1 – 0.9 million
- less than 0.1 million
- no cultivation

GM contamination, illegal plantings and negative agricultural side-effects
1996–2007

5 or more incidents reported (number given)

1 – 4 incidents reported

GM soya

In 2001, Roundup-Ready soya was found in two products on sale in India, despite them having no government import permit.

GM found in organic food

GM soya and maize was found in 44 out of 58 products sold in South Africa as "organic" or "non-GM".

GM papaya

Analysis of papayas from farms in northeast Thailand revealed that they had been contaminated by a GM variety, grown experimentally on a government research station and not licensed for commercial use.

GM found in baby food

Analysis of 20 baby-food products sold in the Philippines in 2001 found traces of GM soya in seven of them.

NORWAY · SWEDEN · FINLAND
14 UK · IRELAND · DENMARK 6 · NETH. · BELGIUM · LUXEMBOURG · GERMANY 15 · CZECH REP. · POLAND · SLOVAKIA · AUSTRIA · HUNGARY 5 · ROMANIA 6 · FRANCE 12 · SWITZ. · SLOVENIA · CROATIA · SERBIA · BULGARIA · ITALY 5 · GREECE · SPAIN · UGAL

MALTA · CYPRUS · KUWAIT · EGYPT · UAE

RUSSIA · CHINA · SOUTH KOREA · JAPAN 9 · TAIWAN

INDIA · THAILAND · PHILIPPINES

SIERRA LEONE · GHANA

SOUTH AFRICA

AUSTRALIA 9

NEW ZEALAND 7

59m 2002 **81m** 2004 **102m** 2006

15 PESTICIDES

PESTICIDES
By share of market
2005

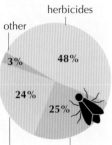

- other 3%
- herbicides 48%
- fungicides 24%
- insecticides 25%

PESTICIDE MARKET GROWTH
1979–2005
US$ billions

- $11.7 — 1980
- $26.4 — 1990
- $31.2 — 2005

PESTICIDES – the collective terms for herbicides, fungicides, insecticides and rodenticides – are manufactured substances used to control weeds, fungi, insects, rodents and other organisms that may reduce crop yields and damage crop quality.

Since the 1950s, sales have dramatically increased and are predicted to continue to do so as agricultural practices in developing countries are modernized. Pesticides are aggressively promoted, in particular in Asia and Latin America. But although they appear to provide a short-term increase in productivity, estimates of their value to agriculture rarely take into account their true cost. This includes damage to the environment and to human health, the development of pesticide-resistant pests, and the expense of testing for residues and disposing of unwanted chemicals.

Pesticides can have a devastating impact on human health. In Benin, for example, where cotton is treated with the insecticide endosulfan, around 70 people died in 1999 because food crops were contaminated, proper protective clothing was unavailable, and farmers were not adequately informed about the products they used.

Pesticides can also have dramatic effects on the environment – poisoning wildlife, contaminating water sources, and passing through the food chain, causing damage along the way. Farmers become trapped on the vicious "pesticides treadmill" – spraying with pesticides destroys the pests' natural enemies, and increases the number of pest outbreaks, as a result of which the farmer uses more pesticides, with the associated negative consequences.

Despite the potentially damaging effects of these chemicals, it is difficult to obtain information about their use, with no effective data-collection system in place.

The manufacture and sale of pesticides is dominated by six companies, who between them accounted for 77 percent of the total global pesticides market in 2004. These companies are also fundamentally changing the nature of agriculture through the promotion of genetically modified (GM) crops designed to withstand herbicides, thereby encouraging the purchase of the chemicals they sell. The control the vast majority of commercialize GM seeds and are continuing to expand i developing countries, where many of th deaths of agricultural workers from exposure t pesticides occur.

Nicaraguans awarded damages in USA

In 2007, six Nicaraguan banana-plantation workers were awarded $3.2m by a US court. They claimed to have been made sterile in the 1970s by the pesticide Nemagon (DBCP) after multinational plantation owners and a pesticide manufacturer concealed the dangers it posed. This is the first of five lawsuits involving at least 5,000 workers from Central America. The judgement is significant in holding multinational companies accountable in their home country.

USA

JAMAICA
BELIZE
GUATEMALA
HONDURAS
NICARAGUA
COSTA RICA
PANAMA
COLOMBIA
ECUADOR
PERU
DOMINICAN REP.
ST LUCIA
BARBADOS
SURINAME
BRAZIL
PARAGUAY
CHILE
ARGENTINA
URUGUAY

70,000
agricultural
workers
are killed
each year
by
pesticide
poisoning

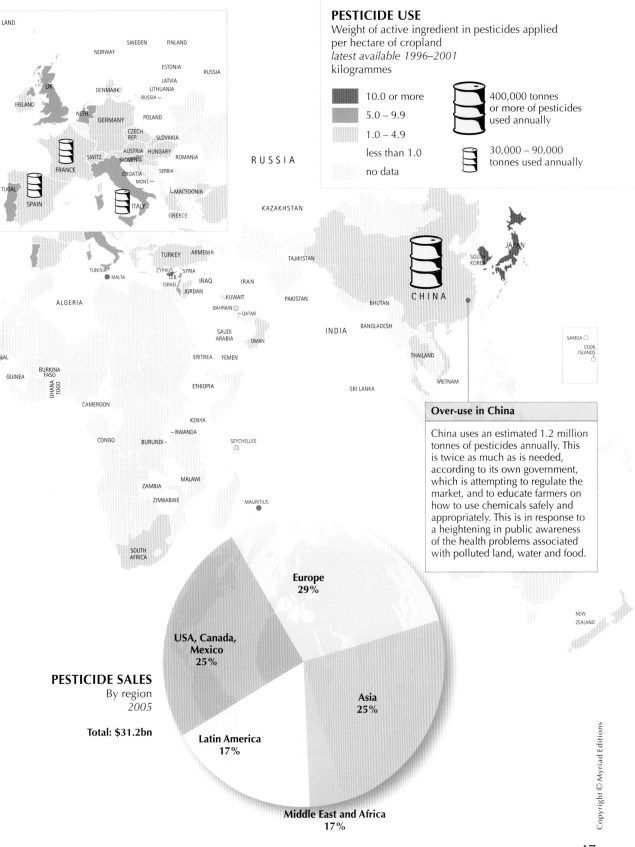

PESTICIDE USE

Weight of active ingredient in pesticides applied per hectare of cropland
latest available 1996–2001
kilogrammes

- 10.0 or more
- 5.0 – 9.9
- 1.0 – 4.9
- less than 1.0
- no data

400,000 tonnes or more of pesticides used annually

30,000 – 90,000 tonnes used annually

Over-use in China

China uses an estimated 1.2 million tonnes of pesticides annually. This is twice as much as is needed, according to its own government, which is attempting to regulate the market, and to educate farmers on how to use chemicals safely and appropriately. This is in response to a heightening in public awareness of the health problems associated with polluted land, water and food.

PESTICIDE SALES

By region
2005

Total: $31.2bn

Europe 29%

USA, Canada, Mexico 25%

Asia 25%

Latin America 17%

Middle East and Africa 17%

16 FERTILIZERS

10
billion tonnes
**of fertilizer
is used
every year
to produce feed
for US livestock**

FERTILIZERS HELP INCREASE and maintain crop yields, and non-organic (chemical) fertilizers played a leading role in the "green revolution" that markedly improved yields in developing countries during the second half of the last century. The total amount used more than quadrupled between 1960 and 1990, and of the three main types, nitrogen fertilizers increased the most.

Extensive and improper use of nitrogen fertilizers is now recognized as having many adverse environmental impacts. Nitrogen can combine with oxygen in seven different ways, six of which cause problems. Washed into rivers and groundwater, it can lead to eutrofication (excessive plant growth and decay) and, in extreme cases, blue baby syndrome (a fatal blood disorder).

Released into the atmosphere, nitrogen contributes both to an increase in ground-level ozone (a major air pollutant), and damage to the stratospheric ozone layer. It also contributes to acid rain, which kills off forests and damages buildings. As a result of industrial pollution and heavy fertilizer use over the last 50 years, a torrent of nitrogen is now falling to the ground.

Nitrogen fertilizer is also recognized as a major contributor to climate change. It requires a significant amount of energy to produce, resulting in the release of carbon dioxide into the atmosphere. And nitrous oxide, released by nitrogen-rich soil, is itself a greenhouse gas, with 300 times the Global Warming Potential (GWP) of carbon dioxide.

**Total:
141.6 million tonnes**

FERTILIZER SHARE
Nitrogen, phosphate
and potash fertilizers used
2002

rest of the world 26%
China 28%
USA 14%
India 11%
Brazil 5%
France 3%
Australia 2%
Canada 2%
Germany 2%
Indonesia 2%
Pakistan 2%
Spain 2%

NON-ORGANIC FERTILIZERS

Total weight of nitrogen, phosphate and potash fertilizers used *2002* kg per hectare of arable land

- 400 or more
- 200 – 399
- 100 – 199
- 10 – 99
- fewer than 10
- no data

Change in fertilizer use per hectare
1990–2002

- ⬆ increased by 100% or more
- ⬇ decreased by 50% or more

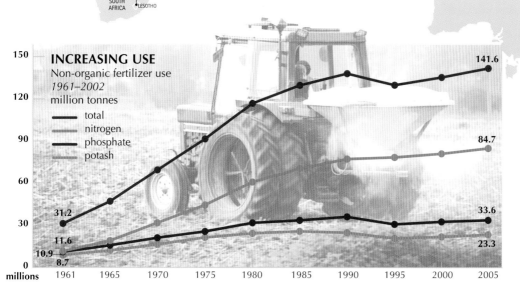

INCREASING USE

Non-organic fertilizer use
1961–2002
million tonnes

- total
- nitrogen
- phosphate
- potash

	1961									2005
total	31.2									141.6
nitrogen	11.6									84.7
phosphate	10.9									33.6
potash	8.7									23.3

millions 1961 1965 1970 1975 1980 1985 1990 1995 2000 2005

17 WORKING THE LAND

DECLINING IMPORTANCE

Agricultural labour force as percentage of world labour force
1950–2010 projected

67%
56%
49%
41%

1950
1970
1990
2010

CANADA

USA

BERMUDA

MEXICO

BAHAMAS

CAYMAN IS.   CUBA   DOMINICAN
REP.   PUERTO RICO

JAMAICA   HAITI   VIRGIN IS. (UK)

BELIZE   ANGUILA
VIRGIN IS. (US)   ANTIGUA & BARBUDA

GUATEMALA   HONDURAS   ST KITTS & NEVIS   GUADELOUPE
DOMINICA

EL SALVADOR   NICARAGUA   ARUBA   GRENADA   ST LUCIA   MARTINIQU
BARBADOS

COSTA RICA   ST VINCENT & GRENAD
TRINIDAD & TOBAGO

PANAMA   VENEZUELA   GUYANA
SURINAME

COLOMBIA   FRENCH GUIANA

ECUADOR

PERU

BRAZIL

BOLIVIA

PARAGUAY

CHILE   ARGENTINA

URUGUAY

THE LAND is the main source of both food and income for just under half the people in the world. And, despite rapid urbanization, which means that the agricultural sector is declining as a percentage of the total labour force, the number of people working on the land is actually increasing.

The number of women involved in agriculture also appears to be going up – although this may be because women's contribution to subsistence farming is becoming more widely recognized. Children, too, play an important part in tending family land, and also make up a sizable proportion of the commercial labour force – around 25 percent of sugar-cane workers in northeastern Brazil, for example. In South Asia and Latin America many children work as bonded labourers to repay family debts.

In developing countries, human labour, plus some equipment and animal power, is the energy source for growing food. In parts of Africa this vital supply of energy, along with knowledge passed on through generations, is being devastated by AIDS – a situation predicted to have a disastrous affect on food security in many countries.

In industrialized countries, where much of the cultivation and harvesting is done by machinery, the percentage of the labour force employed in agriculture declined dramatically during the 20th century. But although fewer people are working *on* the land, many more are working *for* the land – making fertilizers, agrochemicals, tractors, buildings, pharmaceuticals. The role of this "hidden" agricultural labour force is to increase the productivity of the remaining land workers.

Many countries are turning from labour-intensive methods to the use of machines, often in order to produce crops for export. But where the process of replacing human labour with machines has not been undertaken as part of a larger economic plan, it has led to high levels of rural unemployment and the inevitable transformation of agricultural labourers into the urban poor.

30%
of
coffee pickers
are children at
peak
harvest time
in Kenya

INCREASING NUMBERS

Men and women as proportion of world agricultural labor force
1950–2010 projected

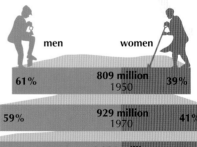

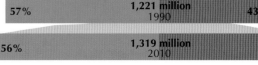

men   women

61%   809 million   39%
1950

59%   929 million   41%
1970

57%   1,221 million   43%
1990

56%   1,319 million   4
2010

AGRICULTURAL WORKERS

as percentage of economically active population
2010 projected

- 70% or more
- 50% – 69%
- 30% – 49%
- 10% – 29%
- less than 10%
- no data

more than 50%
of agricultural workforce
are women

ICELAND
NORWAY
FINLAND
SWEDEN
ESTONIA
LATVIA
RUSSIA –
LITHUANIA
UK
DENMARK
IRELAND
NETH.
GERMANY
POLAND
BELARUS
BEL.
CZ. REP.
SL.
UKRAINE
LUX.
FRANCE
SWITZ.
AUS.
HUN.
SL.
MOLDOVA
ROM.
S. MARINO
ITALY
CRO.
SERB.
BUL.
PORTUGAL
SPAIN
ANDORRA
M.–
ALB.
MAC.
GREECE
BOSNIA-
HERZEGOVINA
MALTA
GIBRALTAR
TUNISIA
MOROCCO
ALGERIA
LIBYA
GEORGIA
ARMENIA
AZER.
TURKEY
CYPRUS
LEB.–
ISRAEL –
SYRIA
IRAQ
JORDAN
KUWAIT
BAHRAIN
QATAR
UAE
IRAN
OMAN
SAUDI
ARABIA
YEMEN
EGYPT
ERITREA
DJIBOUTI
SUDAN
CHAD
ETHIOPIA
SOMALIA
MAURITANIA
MALI
NIGER
BURKINA
FASO
GUINEA
CÔTE
D'IVOIRE
GHANA
TOGO
BENIN
NIGERIA
CAMEROON
CENTRAL
AFRICAN REP.
LIBERIA
EQUATORIAL
GUINEA
SAO TOME
& PRINCIPE
GABON
CONGO
DEMOCRATIC
REPUBLIC OF
CONGO
UGANDA
KENYA
RWANDA
BURUNDI
TANZANIA
SEYCHELLES
ANGOLA
ZAMBIA
MALAWI
COMOROS
MADAGASCAR
MAURITIUS
RÉUNION
ZIMBABWE
NAMIBIA
BOTSWANA
MOZAMBIQUE
SWAZILAND
SOUTH
AFRICA
LESOTHO
ST HELENA

RUSSIA
KAZAKHSTAN
MONGOLIA
UZBEKISTAN
KYRGYZSTAN
TURKMEN.
TAJIKISTAN
AFGHANISTAN
CHINA
NORTH
KOREA
SOUTH
KOREA
JAPAN
PAKISTAN
NEPAL
BHUTAN
INDIA
BANGLADESH
BURMA
LAOS
THAILAND
VIETNAM
SRI LANKA
CAMBODIA
MALDIVES
BRUNEI
MALAYSIA
SINGAPORE
PHILIPPINES
INDONESIA
EAST TIMOR
PAPUA
NEW
GUINEA
AUSTRALIA
NEW
ZEALAND

NORTHERN MARIANA IS.
GUAM
MARSHALL ISLANDS
MICRONESIA,
FED. STATES OF
NAURU
KIRIBATI
TUVALU
SOLOMON
ISLANDS
AMERICAN SAMOA
SAMOA
VANUATU
FIJI
COOK
ISLANDS
NEW
CALEDONIA
TONGA
FRENCH
POLYNESIA
PALAU

IMPACT OF AIDS IN AFRICA
*Estimated loss of
agricultural labour force
2020 projected*

Tanzania	Uganda	Malawi	Kenya	South Africa	Mozambique	Zimbabwe	Botswana	Namibia
–13%	–14%	–14%	–17%	–20%	–20%	–23%	–23%	–26%

15%

of the world's population own almost all the productive land not owned by the state

THE NUMBER OF PEOPLE living on food-productive land, and the amount of land available for food, varies widely around the world. Bhutan has an average of 16 people living on each of its productive arable hectares, while the least densely populated agricultural lands are in the USA, Canada and Australia – so mechanized is their production, and so urbanized are their populations.

In almost all countries where land is not controlled by the state, land ownership is highly concentrated. A small number of people control the way land is used, whether for growing food, for other commercial enterprises, such as forestry, mining or property development, or for growing biofuels.

Land is a prime source of wealth, and access to it is hotly contested. Tenant farmers and peasants have a long tradition of struggling for land rights – against landlords and governments. In many countries, land rights movements call for land reform to reduce hunger and for what the UN terms "food rights". They are often addressing the legacy of invasions and empires – and even the creation of National Parks.

In Australia, two centuries after losing their rights to the invading English, the indigenous people won some back in 1976. In the 1990s the Brazilian Landless Workers Movement (MST) won public support, as well as helping 151,000 people take over 2 million unused acres of land. In India, the Janadesh movement is calling for a Land Commission to resolve land disputes that are preventing people from growing their own food. In 2007, a small land rights movement emerged in China.

Security of tenure is key to improving the living standards of people who depend on the land for their food and livelihood. Without such security, there is little incentive to improve soil, irrigation or livestock. Ownership of land, and investment in improving it, can form a "virtuous circle" essential for economic and social development.

29%

of land in the USA is owned by the government

Brazil – rights for the landless

The Landless Rural Workers' Movement (MST) has 1.5 million members. Founded in 1984, it helps people living in poverty to claim the right to grow food on under-utilized or abandoned land. It is now recognized by government and UN bodies, but is opposed by large landowners.

30%

of agricultural land in Spain is owned by just 52 families

ICELAND
NORWAY   FINLAND
SWEDEN
RUSSIA
ESTONIA
LATVIA
UK   DENMARK   LITHUANIA
RUSSIA
IRELAND   NETH.   GERMANY   POLAND   BELARUS
BEL.   CZ. REP.   SL.   UKRAINE
LUX.   AUS.   HUN.   MOLDOVA
FRANCE   SWITZ.   SL.   ROM.
MONT.   CRO.   B-H   SERB.   BUL.
ALB.   MAC.
PORTUGAL   SPAIN   ITALY   GREECE   TURKEY
TUNISIA   MALTA   CYPRUS   SYRIA
LEB.
ISRAEL   IRAQ
PALESTINE AUTHORITY   JORDAN
MOROCCO
ALGERIA   LIBYA   EGYPT   KUWAIT   BAHRAIN   QATAR   UAE
SAUDI ARABIA   OMAN
MAURITANIA   MALI   NIGER   CHAD   SUDAN   ERITREA   YEMEN
AL   BURKINA FASO
GUINEA   CÔTE D'IVOIRE   NIGERIA   CENTRAL AFRICAN REPUBLIC   ETHIOPIA
ONE   GHANA TOGO BENIN
LIBERIA   CAMEROON
EQUATORIAL GUINEA   UGANDA   SOMALIA
SAO TOME & PRINCIPE   GABON   DEMOCRATIC REPUBLIC OF CONGO   KENYA
CONGO   RWANDA   BURUNDI   TANZANIA   SEYCHELLES
ANGOLA   MALAWI   COMOROS
ZAMBIA   MADAGASCAR
NAMIBIA   ZIMBABWE   BOTSWANA   MOZAMBIQUE   MAURITIUS   RÉUNION
SWAZILAND
SOUTH AFRICA   LESOTHO

RUSSIA
KAZAKHSTAN   MONGOLIA
UZBEKISTAN   KYRGYZSTAN   NORTH KOREA   JAPAN
ARMENIA   AZER.   TURKMEN.   TAJIKISTAN   SOUTH KOREA
GEORGIA   AFGHANISTAN   CHINA
IRAN   NEPAL   BHUTAN
PAKISTAN   INDIA   BANGLADESH   BURMA   LAOS
THAILAND   VIETNAM   PHILIPPINES
CAMBODIA
SRI LANKA
MALDIVES   BRUNEI
MALAYSIA
SINGAPORE
INDONESIA
EAST TIMOR

KIRIBATI
SOLOMON ISLANDS
NEW CALEDONIA   FIJI

AUSTRALIA
PAPUA NEW GUINEA
NEW ZEALAND

India – Janadesh movement

In 2007, 25,000 people marched across India demanding land on which to live and grow food, and highlighting how rural people without formal legal land deeds suffer the worst poverty rates.

South Africa – land and politics

With the election of the ANC in 1994, land rights emerged as central to three political initiatives: to restore lands taken under apartheid; to offer land to the urban poor who want it; and to provide security of tenure for workers in the former "native reserves" or Bantustans.

Australia – aboriginal rights

Since winning the first legal title to land in 1956, Aboriginal Australians have struggled for recognition of their traditional law, as opposed to Australian law derived from the colonial English system. The 1976 Aboriginal Land Rights Act established some basis for claiming land, extended by subsequent law cases.

19 URBAN FARMING

$500 million

worth of
fruit and
vegetables
is produced
by urban farmers
worldwide

AROUND 800 MILLION city dwellers worldwide – including some in industrialized countries – use their agricultural skills to feed themselves and their families. The world's cities are expanding at an ever-increasing rate. People are leaving agricultural regions no longer able to support them in order to find employment in urban areas. Some of the world's largest cities are now to be found in developing countries. However, most urban immigrants arrive to find poverty and malnutrition in place of employment.

As well as growing food for their own consumption, around 200 million also earn a living growing food and rearing livestock to sell at local markets, while a further 150 million are employed as labourers on urban farms. The outskirts of most cities in Africa, Asia and Latin America support thousands of cattle, goats, pigs, chickens and rabbits, and both small and large livestock are also found in inner-city areas. When Hong Kong had an outbreak of avian influenza in 1997, it was revealed by government authorities intent on eradication that over 1 million chickens were housed in residential areas.

In times of severe political or economic crisis, when supply lines or currencies collapse, large cities are particularly vulnerable to food shortages. Increased urban food production is in many cases a response to this problem.

Supplying nutritionally adequate and safe food to city dwellers is a substantial challenge for governments and planners. Urban farming creates employment and income, increases food security and can improve the urban environment, but it faces stiff competition for land from developers. In order to ensure a healthy future for urban small-holdings, policy-makers need a properly integrated policy that anticipates the changing needs of both rural and urban populations, and the links between them. Steps also need to be taken to control pollution, thereby safeguarding the produce of urban agriculture from contamination.

URBANIZATION
Percentage of world population living in cities

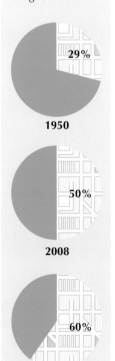

29% 1950

50% 2008

60% 2030 projected

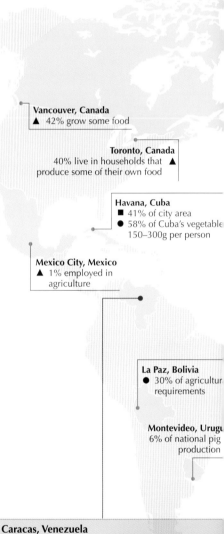

Vancouver, Canada
▲ 42% grow some food

Toronto, Canada
40% live in households that ▲ produce some of their own food

Havana, Cuba
■ 41% of city area
● 58% of Cuba's vegetable 150–300g per person

Mexico City, Mexico
▲ 1% employed in agriculture

La Paz, Bolivia
● 30% of agricultur requirements

Montevideo, Urugu
6% of national pig production

Caracas, Venezuela

In 2003, the government installed 4,000 micro-gardens in poor neighbourhoods of Caracas and started 20 horticultural cooperatives in and around the city.

London, UK

Around 14% of households in London grow some fruit or vegetables. This includes around 30,000 allotment holders, who rent public land in order to grow their own food.

FOOD PRODUCTION IN URBAN AND SUBURBAN AREAS

▲ percentage of inhabitants or households involved in agriculture in urban or suburban area

■ percentage of city area used for agriculture

● percentage of agricultural needs of city met by urban and / or suburban production

London, UK
▲ 14% of households grow vegetables in garden

St Petersburg, Russia
▲ 50% of inhabitants

Moscow, Russia
▲ 65% of families

Shanghai, China
▲ 20% of inhabitants
● 100% of milk
● 90% of eggs
● 60% of vegetables

Beijing, China
14% of population ▲

Germany
5% of population ▲
efit from allotment gardens

Sofia, Bulgaria
▲ 50% households
■ 41% of municipal area

Tokyo, Japan
■ 10% of total area

enegal
of vegetables

Amman, Jordan
▲ 16% of households

Kathmandu, Nepal
▲ 37% of households
● 30% of vegetables

Yaoundé, Cameroon
▲ 35% of inhabitants, 40% of whom also keep livestock

Cairo, Egypt
▲ 16% of households keep animals
■ 8% of city area

Dhaka, Bangladesh
● 80% keep livestock

Cagayan de Oro, Philippines
40% of households ▲
45% of city area ■
70% of fish ●

Ougadoudou, Burkina Faso
% of urban ▲
opulation

Hanoi, Vietnam
■ 18% of urban land
● 44% of food requirements
80% leafy vegetables

Libreville, Gabon
▲ 80% of families

Kampala, Uganda
▲ 36% of families
■ 50% of city area
● 20% of staple foods
● 70% of poultry products

Hyderabad, India
● 6% of milk

Singapore
● 100% of meat
● 25% of vegetables

Accra, Ghana
% of households ▲
involved in subsistence production
% of vegetables ●

Kisangani, Dem Rep Congo
▲ 30% of households

Nairobi, Kenya
▲ 25% – 30% of households
● 50% of food consumed by low-income households

Port Moresby, Papua-New Guinea
80% of households ▲

Brazzaville, Congo
33% of households ▲
65% of marketed ●
vegetables

Dar es Salaam, Tanzania
▲ 37% of families
■ 23% of city area
● almost 30 percent of food supplies

Jakarta, Indonesia
1% of population ▲
9.5% of vegetables ●
20% of fruit ●
18% of food eaten ●
by low-income households

Suva, Fiji
40% of families ▲

Lusaka, Zambia
45% of families ▲

Maputo, Mozambique
▲ 37% of households

Harare, Zimbabwe
80% of all households in summer; ▲
60% in winter; over 33% of households keep livestock
16% of city area ■

Dar-es-Salaam, Tanzania

Nearly 40% of the families in Dar-es-Salaam are dependent on food and income from farming, which covers over 23% of the city area. Urban farmers produce 90% of the leafy vegetables consumed in the city, and also raise livestock, including 6.5 million chickens.

Copyright © Myriad Editions

Fish consumption in wealthy countries between 1997 and 2003 increased by

7%

THE AMOUNT OF FISH CONSUMED varies enormously around the world, depending on availability, income and culture, but it provides 2.8 billion people with at least a fifth of their protein. Only half is eaten fresh; the rest is canned, cured or frozen. A quarter of all fish caught or farmed is used for animal (including fish) feed, and fish oil, and the demand for fish, both from consumers and farmers, is increasing.

Although the quantity of fish caught in the seas and oceans increased steadily between the 1950s and the mid-1990s, it has since levelled off. Three-quarters of fish stocks monitored around the world have been exploited at or beyond sustainable levels, and only careful, coordinated management will enable the world's total fish catch to increase. National governments and international organizations are working on policies to protect stocks, but with no single body controlling fishing in international waters any policy relies on voluntary cooperation from the countries and fishing fleets concerned.

As natural fish stocks decline, demand, especially for non-native fish in industrialized countries, is being met by aquaculture (fish farming), an industry that is growing by nearly 9 percent a year and that now accounts for more than 40 percent of fish eaten around the world. It also provides a third of all fishmeal, the bulk of which is used in the poultry industry. Most aquaculture takes place in low-income countries. As well as being a valuable export, it is increasingly seen as important to domestic food security. However, unregulated aquaculture is leading to contaminants in fish feed being passed down the food chain, and the effluent from fish farms causing damage to the environment and spreading diseases into the wild population.

Inland waters, mainly freshwater, account for only 7 percent of the world's fish catch, but this valuable source of protein in developing countries is especially vulnerable to over-fishing and to damage by effluent and agricultural chemicals.

WHERE FISH COMES FROM
2006

**Total:
142 million tonnes**

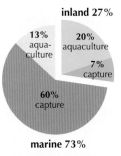

inland 27%

13% aquaculture

20% aquaculture

7% capture

60% capture

marine 73%

WHERE IT GOES
2006

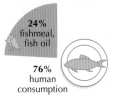

24% fishmeal, fish oil

76% human consumption

China's fish production

In 2005, China accounted for 18% of the global fish catch, and 35% of all aquaculture. Most of the fish is for domestic consumption or for use as animal feed.

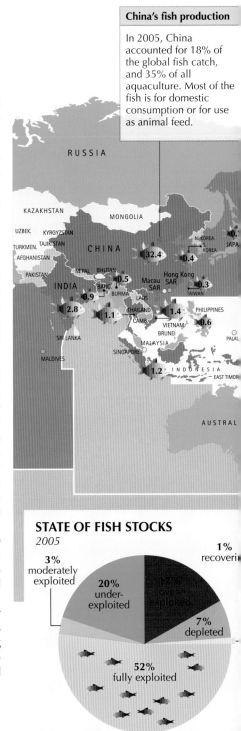

STATE OF FISH STOCKS
2005

3% moderately exploited

20% under-exploited

1% recoveri

17% over-exploited

7% depleted

52% fully exploited

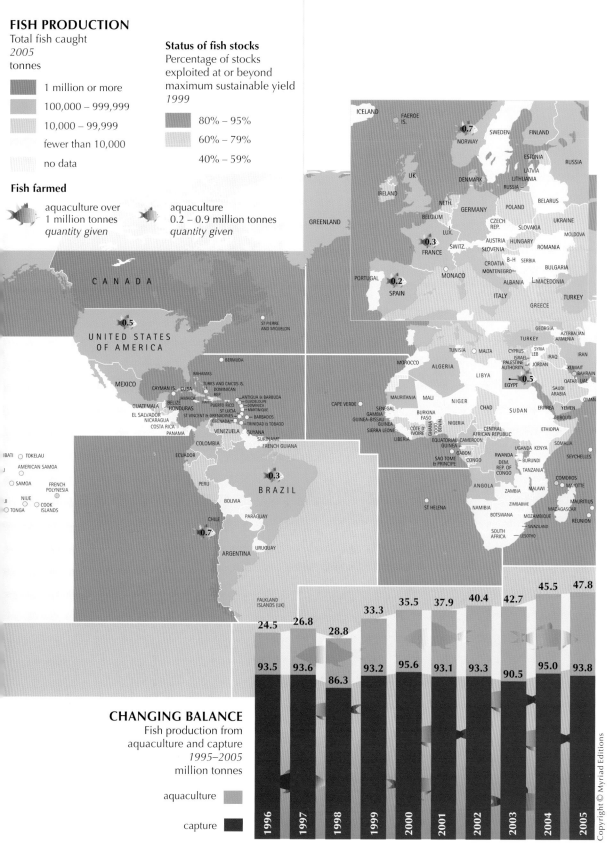

FISH PRODUCTION

Total fish caught
2005
tonnes

- 1 million or more
- 100,000 – 999,999
- 10,000 – 99,999
- fewer than 10,000
- no data

Status of fish stocks

Percentage of stocks
exploited at or beyond
maximum sustainable yield
1999

- 80% – 95%
- 60% – 79%
- 40% – 59%

Fish farmed

aquaculture over
1 million tonnes
quantity given

aquaculture
0.2 – 0.9 million tonnes
quantity given

CHANGING BALANCE

Fish production from
aquaculture and capture
1995–2005
million tonnes

- aquaculture
- capture

Year	aquaculture	capture
1996	24.5	93.5
1997	26.8	93.6
1998	28.8	86.3
1999	33.3	93.2
2000	35.5	95.6
2001	37.9	93.1
2002	40.4	93.3
2003	42.7	90.5
2004	45.5	95.0
2005	47.8	93.8

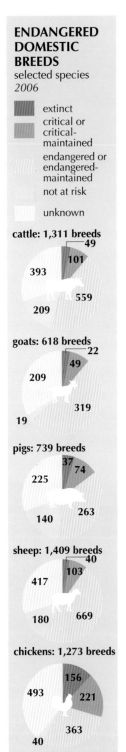

ENDANGERED DOMESTIC BREEDS
selected species
2006

- extinct
- critical or critical-maintained
- endangered or endangered-maintained
- not at risk
- unknown

cattle: 1,311 breeds
49
101
393
559
209

goats: 618 breeds
22
49
209
319
19

pigs: 739 breeds
37
74
225
263
140

sheep: 1,409 breeds
40
103
417
669
180

chickens: 1,273 breeds
156
493
221
363
40

AGRICULTURAL BIODIVERSITY includes not only the animals and plants used for food, but the diversity of species that support food production – micro-organisms in the soil, crop pollinators, pest-predators – and the wider environment within which the agricultural ecosystem is located.

The genetic diversity of our food has arisen from a 10,000-year process in which wild species have been selected and bred to create the domesticated varieties used today. The regions where these developments took place are defined as centres of diversity of specific crops and related wild species. Such diversity is important because it provides a pool of genes that have developed natural resistance to pests and other environmental stress over time, and will help to ensure the future survival of key food crops. Relying on a single variety of crop to provide food makes a population vulnerable to pests and disease.

But the genetic diversification of food crops and animal breeds is diminishing rapidly. At the beginning of the 21st century it is estimated that only 10 percent of the variety of crops that have been developed in the past are still being farmed, with many local varieties being replaced by a small number of improved varieties, often involving non-native plants.

Around 70 percent of the world's rural poor rely for their livelihood on the health of their livestock, but the genetic diversity of domestic breeds is threatened by increasing reliance on a small number of high-output breeds. At least one breed has become extinct every month over the last seven years, and a fifth of domestic breeds are considered at risk.

In regions relatively untouched by industrial farming, a huge variety of crops is still in use. In Peru, for example, 3,000 varieties of potato are cultivated. But many areas of genetic diversity are under threat from "contamination" and domination by introduced varieties, including genetically modified crops. So although genetic diversity is best maintained in the field, gene banks – such as those of the Svalbard Global Seed Vault, opened early in 2008 – conserve genetic material artificially, as a backup.

VEGETABLES AND FRUIT
Status of original varieties in USA

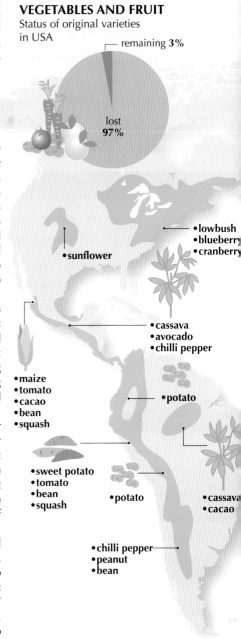

remaining 3%
lost 97%

- sunflower
- lowbush
- blueberry
- cranberry
- cassava
- avocado
- chilli pepper
- maize
- tomato
- cacao
- bean
- squash
- potato
- sweet potato
- tomato
- bean
- squash
- potato
- cassava
- cacao
- chilli pepper
- peanut
- bean

GENETIC ORIGINS

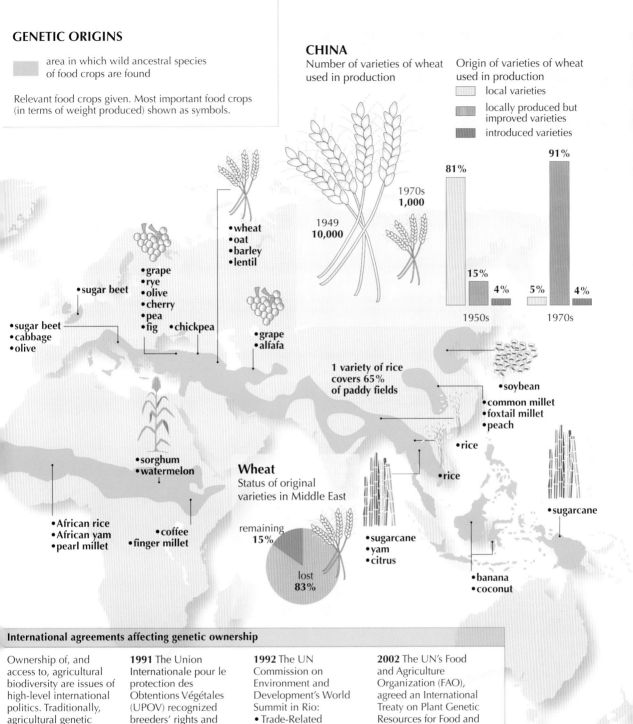

area in which wild ancestral species of food crops are found

Relevant food crops given. Most important food crops (in terms of weight produced) shown as symbols.

CHINA

Number of varieties of wheat used in production

Origin of varieties of wheat used in production

local varieties

locally produced but improved varieties

introduced varieties

81%

91%

1970s
1,000

1949
10,000

15%

4%

5%

4%

1950s

1970s

• wheat
• oat
• barley
• lentil

• grape
• rye
• olive
• cherry
• pea
• fig   • chickpea

• sugar beet

• sugar beet
• cabbage
• olive

• grape
• alfafa

1 variety of rice covers 65% of paddy fields

• soybean

• common millet
• foxtail millet
• peach

• rice

• rice

• sorghum
• watermelon

Wheat
Status of original varieties in Middle East

remaining
15%

lost
83%

• sugarcane
• yam
• citrus

• sugarcane

• African rice
• African yam
• pearl millet

• coffee
• finger millet

• banana
• coconut

International agreements affecting genetic ownership

Ownership of, and access to, agricultural biodiversity are issues of high-level international politics. Traditionally, agricultural genetic diversity has been a shared resource, and farmers have been free to save seeds to use in future plantings, but a series of agreements from the 1990s has jeopardized this free access to food crops.

1991 The Union Internationale pour le protection des Obtentions Végétales (UPOV) recognized breeders' rights and gave legal ownership of industrialized seeds to the companies that developed them.

1992 The UN Commission on Environment and Development's World Summit in Rio:
• Trade-Related Intellectual Property Rights agreement extends ownership to living forms
• Convention on Biological Diversity recognized national sovereignty over key genetic resources.

2002 The UN's Food and Agriculture Organization (FAO), agreed an International Treaty on Plant Genetic Resources for Food and Agriculture, allowing common shared access to a limited number of important crop varieties.

22 ORGANIC FARMING

THE GLOBAL TREND towards sustainable practices in agriculture has been termed "the real green revolution", as a contrast to the "green revolution" of the early 1960s, which saw an increase in mechanized, high-input agriculture.

The real green revolution encourages biodiversity, local self-reliance and organic methods. It is partly fuelled by growing consumer demand in the industrialized countries for organic produce, but is also a response to the environmental problems that have developed as a result of the drive to intensify production that has led to the use of excessive pesticides and fertilizers.

Much of the world is already farmed organically, by people in the developing world using traditional methods of cultivation. And while agrochemical companies are encouraging farmers to use chemicals, research is showing how organic composts can also dramatically increase yields. Organically enriched soil holds more moisture, enabling vegetables to be grown even during dry periods.

Many of the techniques devised by organic farmers have now been adopted by conventional farmers, including the "community ecology" approach to controlling pests, which encourages natural predators.

Certain countries, such as Cuba, are leading the world in their adoption of organic methods. Since the collapse of Cuba's major trading partner, the Soviet Union, in the 1990s, and the consequent loss of income with which to buy agrochemicals, it has, out of necessity, turned to organic farming to feed its people. It organically produces 65 percent of its rice and nearly 50 percent of its fresh vegetables, many of the latter produced in an urban environment. Australia has the largest area under organic management, much of it supplying organic beef, while some European countries have the highest percentage of land certified organic. Production is rising fastest in the developing world.

The production of organic meat, dairy produce and eggs is increasing, especially in the industrialized countries. Even in the USA there is a significant rise in organically reared poultry.

INCREASE IN ORGANIC LIVESTOCK IN THE USA
2003–05

Beef cattle

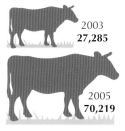

2003
27,285

2005
70,219

Pigs

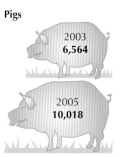

2003
6,564

2005
10,018

Poultry

2003
8.8 million

2005
13.4 million

CANADA

USA

MEXICO

CUBA

JAMAICA

BELIZE

GUATEMALA   HONDURAS
EL SALVADOR   NICARAGUA

DOMINICAN REP.

COSTA RICA
PANAMA

TRINIDAD & TOBAGO

VENEZUELA

GUYANA

COLOMBIA

ECUADOR

PERU

BRAZIL

BOLIVIA

PARAGUAY

CHILE

ARGENTINA   URUGUAY

INCREASE IN ORGANIC LAND
1995–2005
square kilometres

in USA

1995
370 sq km

2000
900 sq km

2005
16,203 sq kr

in EU

1995
1,252 sq km

2000
3,944 sq km

2005
63,000 sq k

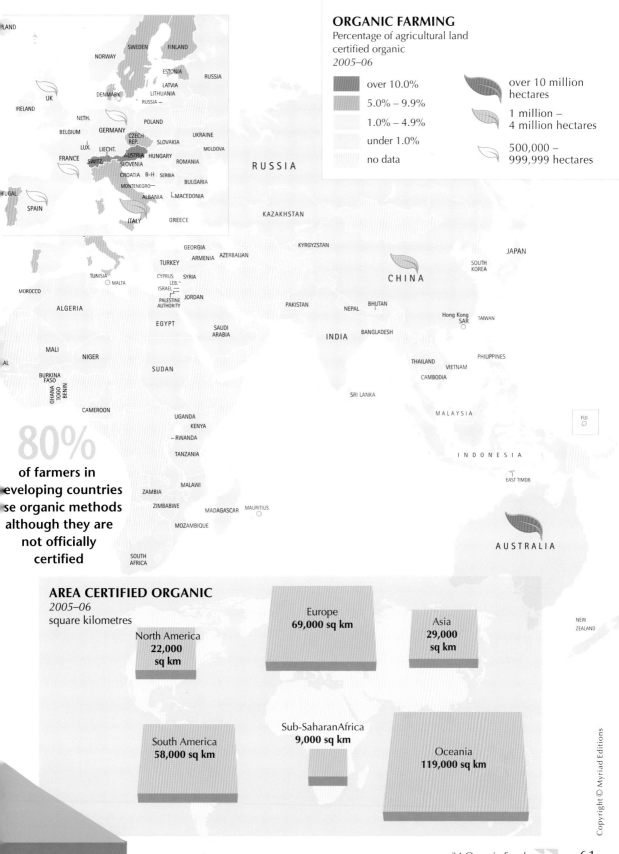

ORGANIC FARMING

Percentage of agricultural land certified organic
2005–06

- over 10.0%
- 5.0% – 9.9%
- 1.0% – 4.9%
- under 1.0%
- no data

- over 10 million hectares
- 1 million – 4 million hectares
- 500,000 – 999,999 hectares

80% of farmers in developing countries use organic methods although they are not officially certified

AREA CERTIFIED ORGANIC
2005–06
square kilometres

North America
22,000 sq km

Europe
69,000 sq km

Asia
29,000 sq km

South America
58,000 sq km

Sub-SaharanAfrica
9,000 sq km

Oceania
119,000 sq km

Copyright © Myriad Editions

34 Organic Food ➤➤

GREENHOUSE GAS EMISSIONS

Agricultural as percentage of total
2007
mid-range estimates

- methane and nitrous oxide
- carbon dioxide

11%
13%
non-agricultural

GLOBAL WARMING POTENTIAL

Selected foods in the UK
2006
kg of CO_2 equivalents per kg of product

AGRICULTURE IS A MAJOR EMITTER of greenhouse gases, with estimates of its contribution to global emissions ranging from 17 to 32 percent. Direct emissions include methane and nitrous oxide released from livestock and from agricultural soil. Indirect emissions include carbon dioxide emitted by agricultural machinery, during the production of fertilizers, and as a result of the deforestation involved in preparing land for crops and pasture.

Projections indicate that without adjustments in agricultural practices, emissions will increase. The world's population is projected to grow by at least one percent a year until 2020, with only a slight slowing thereafter, and more food is needed to support it. In addition, there is a rising demand for meat and dairy products, not only in countries where these have long formed a major part of the diet, but from China, India and the Middle East. The use of nitrogen fertilizers in the cultivation of cattle feed, and the additional emissions from manure are likely to increase nitrous oxide emissions by up to 60 percent by 2030, with increases in East Asia rising even more quickly.

The growing of rice in flooded fields release methane from waterlogged soils, but rice feec a third of the world's population and is a stapl food throughout much of Asia. It is predicte that more land will be used to cultivate rice, s methane emissions are likely to increas accordingly, unless methods of cultivation ar adjusted to include drying out water-logge soils during the fallow season.

Measures to reduce the emission c greenhouse gases from agriculture includ taking better care of soil by tilling it les frequently, incorporating more organic materi and avoiding over-use of nitrogen-base fertilizers. Better management of manure including capturing methane emissions for us as a renewable energy source – and better lan management – including restoring land that ha been degraded, and increasing tree and shru cover on pastures – would all result in a ne decrease of emissions.

A major contribution could be made b people reducing their consumption of meat. every American ate just 5 percent less meat, a estimated 12 million tonnes of carbon-dioxic emissions would be saved.

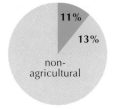

17.4	13.0	6.4	4.6
sheep	beef	pig	poultry

1.3	0.8	0.2
milk	bread, wheat	potato

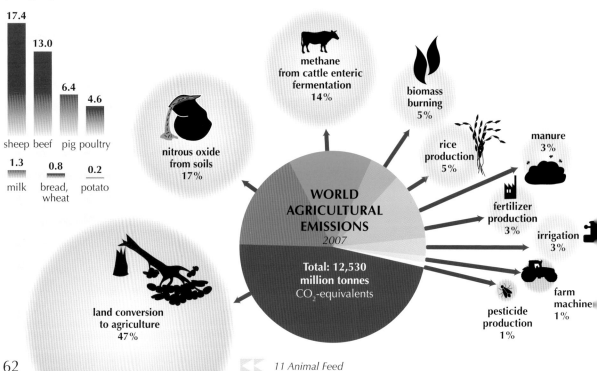

methane from cattle enteric fermentation
14%

biomass burning
5%

nitrous oxide from soils
17%

rice production
5%

manure
3%

WORLD AGRICULTURAL EMISSIONS
2007

Total: 12,530 million tonnes CO_2-equivalents

fertilizer production
3%

irrigation
3%

land conversion to agriculture
47%

pesticide production
1%

farm machine
1%

FROM FARM GATE TO PLATE

The greenhouse gas emissions produced in growing and rearing food is only part of the story. A large proportion of food in the developed world is processed in some way – canned, frozen, or combined with other ingredients to create "ready meals". This uses energy which, unless it comes from a renewable source, results in carbon dioxide emissions.

Food packaging creates further emissions, not only in its manufacture, but by adding to the total weight being transported to retailing and catering outlets. Consumer groups are pressurizing processors and retailers to reduce the amount of packaging used, and Wal-Mart announced early in 2008 that it would try to persuade its 60,000 suppliers to reduce packaging by 5 percent by 2013.

Carbon dioxide is also emitted in the transport of the food – fresh or processed. More and more food is being traded around the world – $852 billion worth in 2005, twice as much as in 1990. Much of this is necessary. Not all countries can meet their own food needs, either in terms of quantity or variety. But in recent years, increasing prosperity in rich countries has given shoppers the purchasing power to attract a continuous supply of "out of season" fruit and vegetables from around the world.

There is no doubt that transporting food by air creates more emissions than transporting it by any other means. A consignment of food sent by ship creates 2 or 3 percent of the emissions of air freighting it. Yet, because of the huge increase in worldwide trade generally, emissions from shipping grew by more than 50 percent in the 20 years up to 2003, and in total have consistently exceeded emissions from aviation.

However, it would appear that, mile for mile, the car journeys people make to purchase their food produces the highest level of emissions. This is hard to assess because it involves so many variables (including the quantity of food purchased and the model of vehicle used) but one estimate equates the emissions created by a 5-mile car journey to purchase groceries, with sending the same groceries 23 miles as part of an air consignment, or 600 miles as part of a truck consignment.

Campaigners and supermarkets in the UK are discussing a system for assessing the greenhouse gas emissions emitted by the production and transportation of food stuffs, which could then be included in labelling, but the complexity of the calculations is proving a sticking point.

COMPARATIVE EMISSIONS

Average grammes of CO_2 emissions from transporting 1 tonne for 1 km

long-haul aircraft
540g–799g

35-tonne lorry
50g–99g

ship
13g–15g

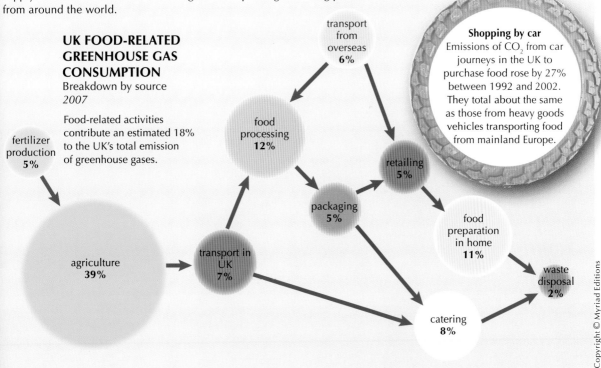

UK FOOD-RELATED GREENHOUSE GAS CONSUMPTION

Breakdown by source
2007

Food-related activities contribute an estimated 18% to the UK's total emission of greenhouse gases.

transport from overseas
6%

fertilizer production
5%

food processing
12%

retailing
5%

packaging
5%

agriculture
39%

transport in UK
7%

food preparation in home
11%

waste disposal
2%

catering
8%

Shopping by car
Emissions of CO_2 from car journeys in the UK to purchase food rose by 27% between 1992 and 2002. They total about the same as those from heavy goods vehicles transporting food from mainland Europe.

PART 3 Trade

Although most food consumed in the world is sourced locally, especially that eaten by poor people, international food trade is a "hot" political topic because it encapsulates the inequity between the industrialized nations and the poorer, predominantly rural countries. Since the 1994 General Agreement on Tariffs and Trade (GATT), agricultural products have been included in trade rules that restrict the capacity of governments financially to support national production. An articulate lobby of developing countries, the G-20, is now able to challenge the powerful USA and EU. Important policy questions have emerged about the impact of trade. Does trade distort or meet needs? Are supply chains becoming less sustainable as they increasingly cross borders? Are diets and well-being improved by more trade? What is fair trade?

Much food trade is controlled and dominated by powerful companies based in rich countries for which food is not the only, or even the main, source of income. Food trade can be beneficial for some countries, but harmful where it undermines food security, or where volatile agricultural prices have a disproportionate effect on economies and livelihoods. This is why the work of the Fairtrade movement, which guarantees vulnerable agricultural communities a stable, minimum price for their products, is so important.

Although the 1994 GATT committed signatory governments to tariff reductions, this is a long process. The EU and USA have historically supported their own farmers, using measures that include tariffs on imports, direct farm payments and indirect subsidies (such as paying a trader to buy and dispose of surplus foodstuffs). Food from subsidizing countries has been "dumped" on developing countries, while they have been locked into requirements to export more, and squeezed, until recently, by declining prices. Trade barriers operated by rich countries cost poor countries $100 billion a year – twice as much as they receive in aid.

Overall, food trade is neither an unmitigated disaster, nor an unmitigated success. It can bring benefits in terms of the interchange of plants, breeds, culinary cultures and techniques. It can also have an adverse effect on economies, the environment and on people's livelihoods. The problem is that for decades, until the vehement opposition that surfaced in Seattle in 1999, it was assumed that the continual extension of trade was a good thing. In this new century, discussions about the future of trade have had to acknowledge the potentially harmful effects of modern food trade's scale, pace and power. The future of food trade will depend on growing anxiety about national supplies and on its environmental impact.

24 TRADE FLOWS

Value of agricultural exports in 2005:

$852

billion

FOOD HAS CROSSED SEAS and continents for millennia. But the scale of food trade today is unprecedented. In 2005, 14 countries accounted for $334 billion of agricultural exports, with exports from and between EU countries amounting to a further $454 billion. The USA, however, changed from being a net exporter of food in 2000, to a net importer in 2005. China is the fastest growing market for agricultural products; it doubled the value of its imports from 2002 to 2005.

A key factor in driving the expansion of international food trade has been regional and global trade agreements. The conventional political view is that expanding food trade is a good thing, but there are also arguments about who wins and loses, whether being export-led or import-dependent threatens food security, and whether developing countries are squeezed by low food-commodity prices.

Such issues have affected the Doha Round of trade talks that began in 2001 in Qatar. The Doha Round highlighted how sensitive food trade is, not just for well-established trading blocs such as the North American Free Trade Agreement and the European Union, but the newly powerful and well-organized G-20 group of developing countries (including China, India, Brazil and South Africa) with a special interest in agriculture.

As governments increasingly turned to biofuels as a source of energy in 2006 and 2007, commodity prices rocketed – good news for exporting countries but bad for importers. Besides the question of who gains financially from food trade, another concern is trade's impact on nutrition. Ever since the 1845–49 Great Irish Famine, political sensitivities have been heightened about the injustice of a country exporting food while its own population goes hungry.

Another concern is trade's environmental impact. This ranges from the energy used to truck, ship and fly food around the globe, to the environmental damage caused by siting intensive production in low-cost countries with weak standards.

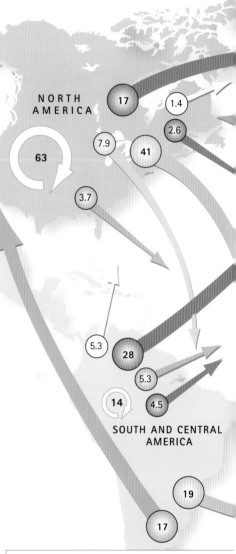

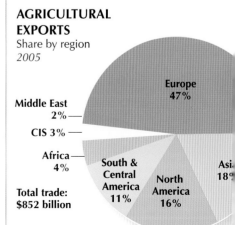

AGRICULTURAL EXPORTS
Share by region
2005

Europe 47%

Middle East 2%

CIS 3%

Africa 4%

South & Central America 11%

North America 16%

Asia 18%

Total trade: $852 billion

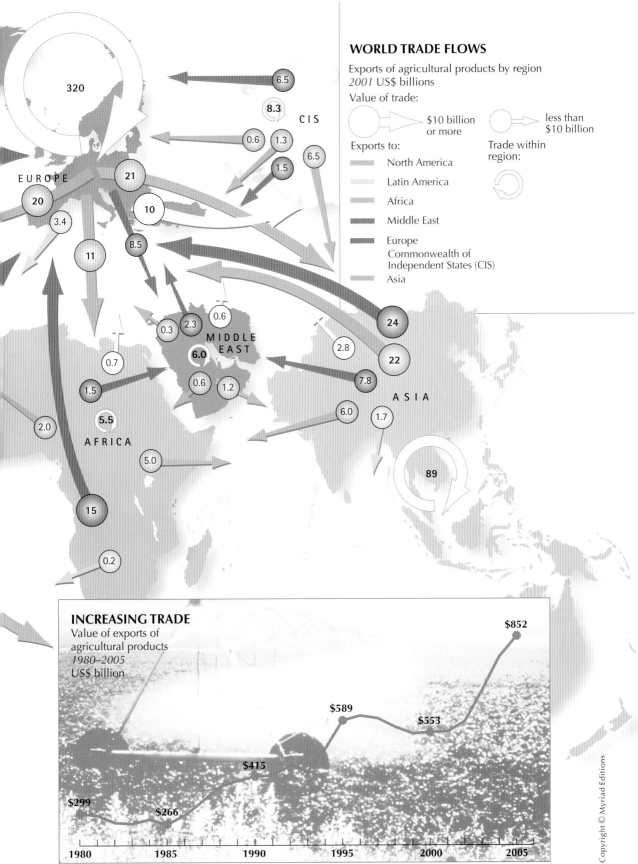

WORLD TRADE FLOWS

Exports of agricultural products by region
2001 US$ billions

Value of trade:

$10 billion or more

less than $10 billion

Exports to:

North America
Latin America
Africa
Middle East
Europe
Commonwealth of Independent States (CIS)
Asia

Trade within region:

320

6.5

8.3

CIS

0.6   1.3

1.5   6.5

EUROPE

20   21

3.4   10

11   8.5

24

0.6

2.3

0.3   MIDDLE EAST

6.0   2.8

22

0.7   7.8

1.5   0.6   1.2

ASIA

5.5

AFRICA   6.0   1.7

5.0

2.0   89

15

0.2

INCREASING TRADE

Value of exports of agricultural products
1980–2005
US$ billion

$852

$589

$553

$415

$299

$266

1980   1985   1990   1995   2000   2005

Copyright © Myriad Editions

67

25 LIVE ANIMAL TRANSPORT

43

million
**animals
are traded
each year**

AROUND 43 MILLION cattle, pigs and sheep are traded across the world each year. Millions more are transported over long distances within such countries as Australia and the USA.

Australia exports around 4 million live sheep each year to the Middle East and over 600,000 cattle to Southeast Asia and the Middle East, mainly to meet the demand for live animals to be slaughtered according to halal procedures, under which the animals are usually not pre-stunned. Opponents of the trade point out that live transport involves immense suffering for these animals and is unnecessary, given that meat slaughtered according to halal procedures in Australia is also deemed acceptable in Islamic countries. In 2006, around 36,000 sheep died of disease and failure to eat during the long journey to the Middle East, which may have involved lengthy travel across Australia to reach a port, a sea crossing of up to three weeks, and an unspecified period of time in a feedlot awaiting slaughter.

In North America, animals are bought an sold across borders, as traders aim to get th best return on their investment. In 2006, th USA imported 2.3 million cattle an 8.8 million pigs, mainly from Canada an Mexico. Within the USA, animals ar transported long distances from where they ar reared to where they are fattened an slaughtered. Many pigs, for example, are ser from the farm of origin in North Carolina to b fattened in Iowa, a journey of 1,000 mile: From there, they are often sent to California fc slaughter, a journey of another 1,700 miles. I Canada, cattle are transported all the way fror the west to slaughterhouses and feedlots i Ontario and Quebec. These journeys can tak over 60 hours.

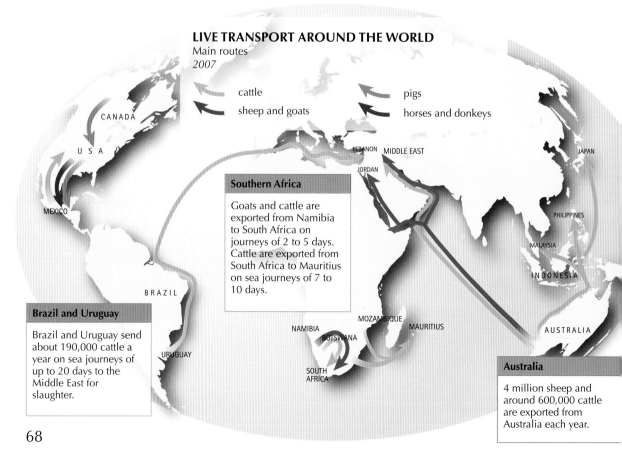

LIVE TRANSPORT AROUND THE WORLD
Main routes
2007

cattle

sheep and goats

pigs

horses and donkeys

Southern Africa

Goats and cattle are exported from Namibia to South Africa on journeys of 2 to 5 days. Cattle are exported from South Africa to Mauritius on sea journeys of 7 to 10 days.

Brazil and Uruguay

Brazil and Uruguay send about 190,000 cattle a year on sea journeys of up to 20 days to the Middle East for slaughter.

Australia

4 million sheep and around 600,000 cattle are exported from Australia each year.

Each year around 6 million animals are transported around Europe on journeys as long as 40 hours or more. Overcrowding, high summer temperatures, deprivation of water, food and rest, and lack of proper ventilation in many vehicles, lead to the animals becoming exhausted, dehydrated and stressed. Some are injured, others collapse. Many die.

Opponents of this trade argue that animals should be slaughtered near to where they were reared, and that the meat should then be transported.

Most trade is from northern to southern Europe but eastern Europe is increasingly becoming both a destination for, and source of, live animals. There are a number of reasons why transporting live animals can be commercially advantageous. Animals (other than cattle) slaughtered in France and Italy, for example, can be described as "home-killed" or "home produced", thereby attracting a premium price. The relatively strict anti-pollution laws in the Netherlands mean that some of the millions of piglets born there each year are sent for fattening to other countries, and the demand for veal leads to the import of young calves.

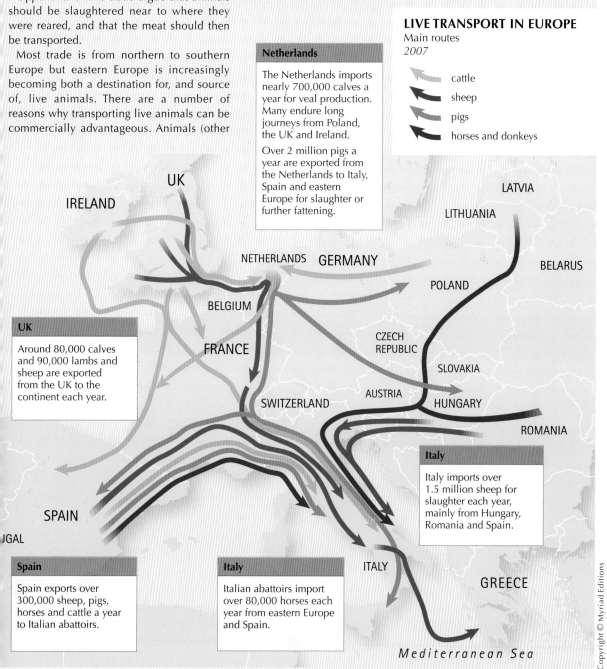

LIVE TRANSPORT IN EUROPE
Main routes
2007

cattle
sheep
pigs
horses and donkeys

Netherlands

The Netherlands imports nearly 700,000 calves a year for veal production. Many endure long journeys from Poland, the UK and Ireland.

Over 2 million pigs a year are exported from the Netherlands to Italy, Spain and eastern Europe for slaughter or further fattening.

UK

Around 80,000 calves and 90,000 lambs and sheep are exported from the UK to the continent each year.

Italy

Italy imports over 1.5 million sheep for slaughter each year, mainly from Hungary, Romania and Spain.

Spain

Spain exports over 300,000 sheep, pigs, horses and cattle a year to Italian abattoirs.

Italy

Italian abattoirs import over 80,000 horses each year from eastern Europe and Spain.

IRELAND
UK
NETHERLANDS
GERMANY
LATVIA
LITHUANIA
BELARUS
POLAND
BELGIUM
CZECH REPUBLIC
FRANCE
SLOVAKIA
AUSTRIA
SWITZERLAND
HUNGARY
ROMANIA
SPAIN
PORTUGAL
ITALY
GREECE

Mediterranean Sea

26 SUBSIDIZED TRADE

SHARE OF SUBSIDY

Share of total farm subsidy
2006 US$

GLOBAL TRADE is not conducted on a level playing field. Governments use various means to support their own agriculture and manufacturing industries by shaping exports and imports. Developing countries often complain that food from high-subsidizing countries is "dumped" in their markets. They calculate that barriers put in place by rich countries cost poor countries $100 billion a year – twice as much as they receive in aid.

Financial support for agriculture includes tariffs (taxes on imported goods), direct subsidies (money paid to the farmer for goods produced), and indirect subsidies (paying a trader to buy and dispose of products that may be surplus to requirement Export restitution reimburses traders who pay high price for a domestic product, but sell it for less on the world market.

From the 1940s, governments gave financia incentives to support home production, bu since the mid-1970s subsidies have bee considered a limitation on "free trade". Th latter policy approach was enshrined in th General Agreement on Tariffs and Trade (GATT signed by over 100 countries in 1994. Onc China signed in 2001, hostility to subsidie became largely accepted. By 2007, 15 countries were signatories.

International efforts to persuade governmen to reduce financial support for farmers hav been fairly successful, but the rate of declin has slowed, as governments have switche support mechanisms. The Producer Subsid

others 1%
Switzerland 2%
Mexico 3%
Canada 3%
Turkey 4%
South Korea 9%
USA 11%
Japan 15%
European Union 52%

Total: $267.7m

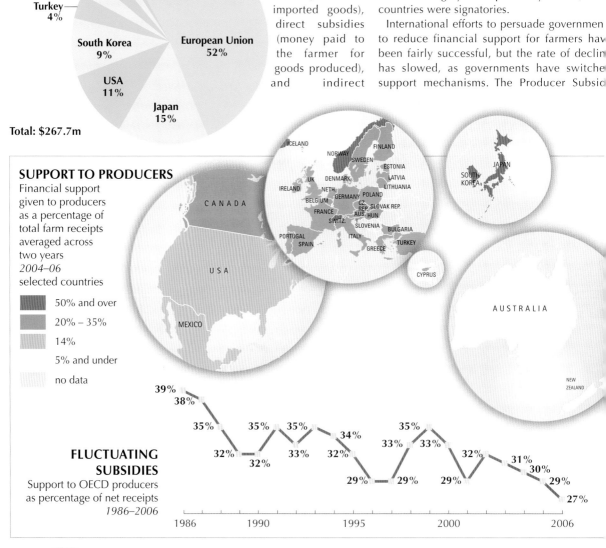

SUPPORT TO PRODUCERS

Financial support given to producers as a percentage of total farm receipts averaged across two years
2004–06
selected countries

- 50% and over
- 20% – 35%
- 14%
- 5% and under
- no data

FLUCTUATING SUBSIDIES

Support to OECD producers as percentage of net receipts
1986–2006

39% 38% 35% 32% 32% 35% 35% 33% 32% 34% 29% 33% 29% 35% 33% 29% 32% 31% 30% 29% 27%

1986   1990   1995   2000   2006

stimate (PSE), a measure of the proportion of arm income that comes from subsidies, shows hat the 30 OECD member countries have educed their farm supports since the mid-1980s. This does not mean, however, that hey no longer support their farmers. The EU as shifted from paying farmers not to grow ood through "set-aside" schemes, to paying hem to protect and enhance the environment. n the USA, up to 7 percent of all support in the early 2000s was on conservation projects. Worried about oil security, governments are now subsidizing farmers to grow biofuels, adding a new dimension to subsidy debates.

Environmentalists have criticized the environmental impact of subsidized farming: intensification, fertilizer run-offs, residues from pesticides and inefficient energy use. Less attention has been paid to the nutritional impact of subsidies. Big recipients are unhealthy foods such as sugar and dairy fats. Between 1986 and 2006, subsidies for milk, eggs, maize, wheat, other grains, soybeans and rapeseed fell by more than half, but protection for rice and sugar received much smaller cuts. It is often forgotten that not only farmers, but large companies receive food subsidies.

TOP TEN RECIPIENTS OF EU SUBSIDIES IN UK
2004–05

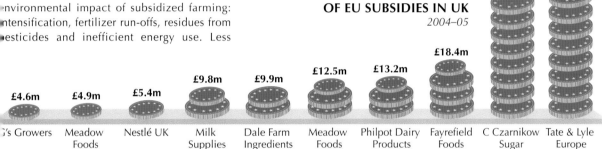

£4.6m	£4.9m	£5.4m	£9.8m	£9.9m	£12.5m	£13.2m	£18.4m	£39.4m	£124m
G's Growers	Meadow Foods	Nestlé UK	Milk Supplies	Dale Farm Ingredients	Meadow Foods	Philpot Dairy Products	Fayrefield Foods Ireland	C Czarnikow Sugar	Tate & Lyle Europe

MARKET PRICE SUPPORT
Percentage support by commodity 1986–88 and 2004–06

■ 1986–88
■ 2004–06

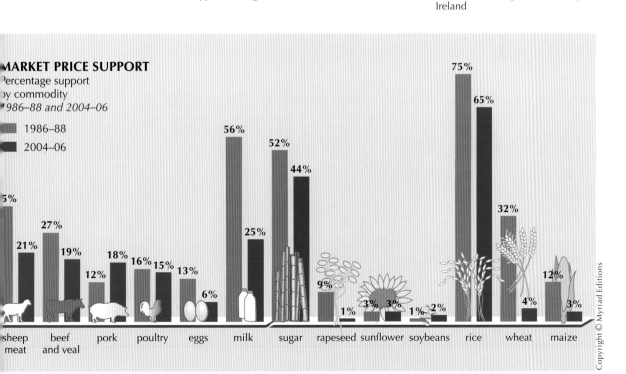

	sheep meat	beef and veal	pork	poultry	eggs	milk	sugar	rapeseed	sunflower	soybeans	rice	wheat	maize
1986–88	5%	27%	12%	16%	13%	56%	52%	9%	3%	1%	75%	32%	12%
2004–06	21%	19%	18%	15%	6%	25%	44%	1%	3%	2%	65%	4%	3%

Copyright © Myriad Editions

27 TRADE DISPUTES

THE BATTLE to secure markets for the increasing amount of food traded around the world frequently results in conflicts of interest between countries, and between the various regional trading blocs. Regional trade deals can be very powerful. They include the 1994 North American Free Trade Agreement (USA, Canada and Mexico) and the European Union (founded by six countries in 1957, and totalling 27 countries by 2007). However, over these regional blocs sits the 1994 General Agreement on Tariffs and Trade (GATT) the global trade deal that created the World Trade Organization (WTO) in 1994 and brought food under world trade rules. The Agreement on Agriculture (AoA), part of the GATT, promoted trade liberalization through reductions in agricultural subsidies, tariffs and import quotas.

Most disputes are settled between the countries or trade blocs involved. In some cases, however, a ruling is sought from the World Trade Organization (WTO), and a system for dispute settlement comes into play. Countries have to follow a process, with binding rulings, that normally takes about [a] year.

The reasons for trade disputes vary. Ground given include: dumping surplus products belo cost price, quality issues, inspection and ta systems, the material specifications of product and copyright and patent issues.

Food features heavily in global and bilater disputes. Products complained about rang from apples to wine, with the mo complained-about foods being bananas, ric poultry and salmon.

In recent years, several trade disputes hav arisen when one country or trading bloc refuse to allow the import of food produced b another on grounds of public health and safet In such cases, the WTO dispute settleme panel is required to refer to standards for foo safety established by the Codex Alimentariu Commission, unless they have more stringe rules that can be backed up scientifically. Thi quite clearly, tilts the scales in favour of thos nations with strong scientific establishments.

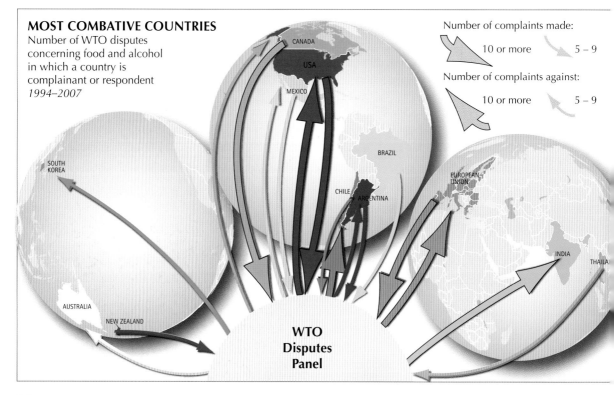

MOST COMBATIVE COUNTRIES
Number of WTO disputes concerning food and alcohol in which a country is complainant or respondent
1994–2007

Number of complaints made:
10 or more   5 – 9

Number of complaints against:
10 or more   5 – 9

CANADA
USA
MEXICO
BRAZIL
SOUTH KOREA
CHILE ARGENTINA
EUROPEAN UNION
INDIA
THAILA
AUSTRALIA
NEW ZEALAND

WTO Disputes Panel

THE BANANA DISPUTE

The banana trade is a multi-million-dollar business, with over a quarter of all banana exports going to the European Union (EU), and a similar amount to the USA. The industrial-scale production methods of multinationals such as Chiquita, Dole, Del Monte, Noboa and Fyffes enable them to produce some of the cheapest bananas on the world market, and to dominate world trade.

In 1993, the European Union sought to protect small-scale banana producers in its former colonies in Africa and the Caribbean (the ACP countries) by imposing tariffs and quotas on bananas imported from other countries. The USA, persuaded of the need to protect its commercial interests in Central and Latin America, complained to the WTO in 1995, in conjunction with other countries affected by the tariffs.

A dispute procedure was put in place that stretched over six years. During that time the USA was granted leave to impose import duties totalling $191 million on goods from EU countries, damaging many European small businesses.

In 2001, the WTO brokered an uneasy settlement. Following a transition period, which ended in 2005, the EU is allowed to import a duty-free quota of 775,000 tonnes of bananas from ACP suppliers, with all other banana imports attracting a tariff. In 2006, the EU set the tariff at €176 per tonne, but this is considered by some countries to be too high, and a request was made to the WTO in 2007 to establish a Compliance Panel to adjudicate on the matter.

80%
of bananas
are traded
by

5

companies

EXPORT SHARE
of bananas
2004

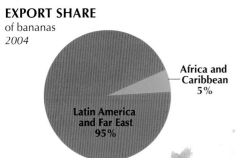

Africa and Caribbean 5%

Latin America and Far East 95%

IMPORT SHARE
of bananas
2004

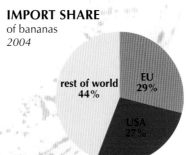

rest of world 44%

EU 29%

USA 27%

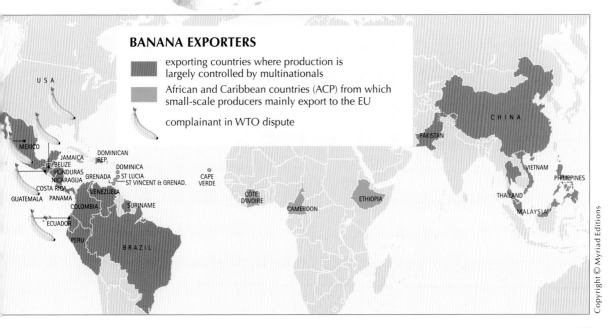

BANANA EXPORTERS

- exporting countries where production is largely controlled by multinationals
- African and Caribbean countries (ACP) from which small-scale producers mainly export to the EU
- complainant in WTO dispute

USA
MEXICO
JAMAICA
BELIZE
HONDURAS
NICARAGUA
COSTA RICA
GUATEMALA
PANAMA
DOMINICAN REP.
DOMINICA
GRENADA
ST LUCIA
ST VINCENT & GRENAD.
VENEZUELA
COLOMBIA
SURINAME
ECUADOR
PERU
BRAZIL
CAPE VERDE
CÔTE D'IVOIRE
CAMEROON
ETHIOPIA
PAKISTAN
CHINA
VIETNAM
PHILIPPINES
THAILAND
MALAYSIA

78%

of all food traded originates from just

20

countries

**FOOD TRADED
INTERNATIONALLY**
As a proportion of
total food sold
2005

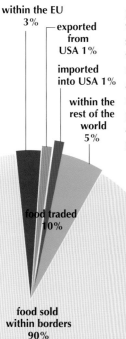

within the EU
3%
— exported
from
USA 1%

imported
into USA 1%

within the
rest of the
world
5%

food traded
10%

food sold
within borders
90%

THE WORLD MARKET does not operate in a benign way, for mutual benefit. It is dominated by affluent countries for whom food is not the sole or even a main source of income, while many poorer countries in Central and South America and in Africa are economically dependent on agricultural exports, which, in some instances, account for more than 50 percent of their exports. New Zealand is a rare example of an affluent developed country for which food exports are a significant proportion of its national wealth.

Around 615 million people live in countries that are primarily agricultural – where agriculture contributes at least 30 percent of GDP and employs around 65 percent of the labour force. Most rural people on very poor incomes live a subsistence life. Food trade is only for those producers who have surpluses. The transition from subsistence to surplus represents the transition from survival to development.

Agricultural prices have a disproportionate impact on agriculture-dependent countries. Individual farmers, as well as entire economies, are extremely vulnerable to fluctuations in commodity prices on the world markets. If prices drop, small farmers who lack reserves to tide them over a bad patch are often forced to sell their crop at less than cost price, and lose their livelihoods as a result. If prices rise, that may be good news for the country's economy as a whole, but it is a separate matter as to who makes the money from the trade: grower, processor or trader? Guaranteeing vulnerable agricultural communities a stable, minimum price for agricultural products is at the heart of the Fairtrade movement.

CANADA

USA

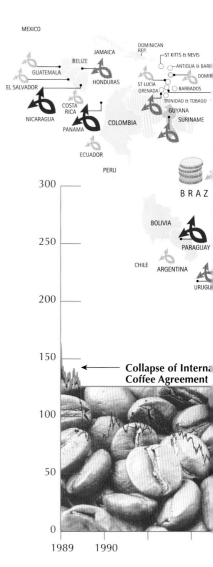

MEXICO

JAMAICA
BELIZE
GUATEMALA
EL SALVADOR
HONDURAS
COSTA
RICA
NICARAGUA
PANAMA
COLOMBIA

DOMINICAN
REP.
ST KITTS & NEVIS
ANTIGUA & BARE
DOMI
ST LUCIA
GRENADA
BARBADOS
TRINIDAD & TOBAGO
GUYANA
SURINAME

ECUADOR

PERU

BRAZ

BOLIVIA

PARAGUAY

CHILE
ARGENTINA

URUGU

300

250

200

150
← **Collapse of Interna
Coffee Agreement**

100

50

0
1989   1990

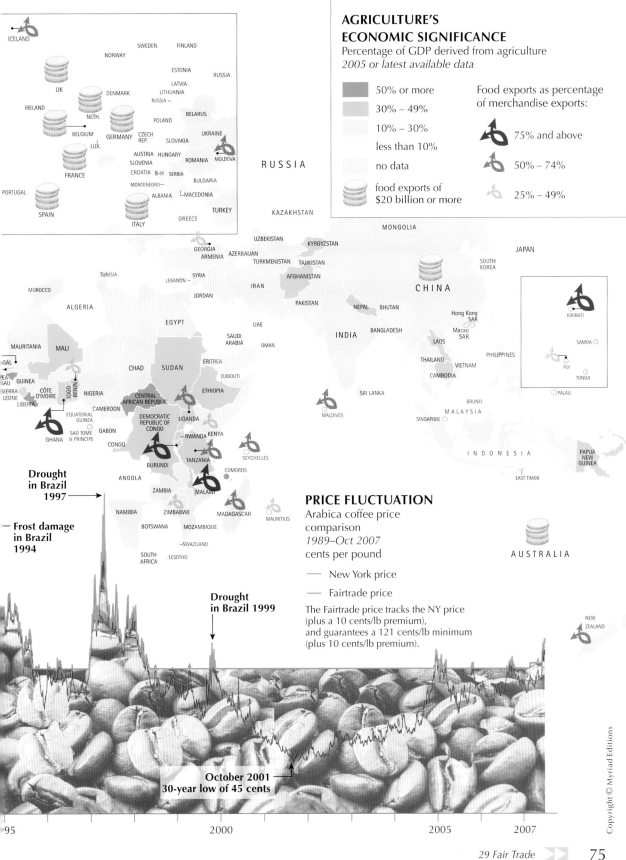

AGRICULTURE'S ECONOMIC SIGNIFICANCE

Percentage of GDP derived from agriculture
2005 or latest available data

- 50% or more
- 30% – 49%
- 10% – 30%
- less than 10%
- no data
- food exports of $20 billion or more

Food exports as percentage of merchandise exports:

- 75% and above
- 50% – 74%
- 25% – 49%

PRICE FLUCTUATION

Arabica coffee price comparison
1989–Oct 2007
cents per pound

— New York price

— Fairtrade price

The Fairtrade price tracks the NY price
(plus a 10 cents/lb premium),
and guarantees a 121 cents/lb minimum
(plus 10 cents/lb premium).

Drought in Brazil 1997

Frost damage in Brazil 1994

Drought in Brazil 1999

October 2001 30-year low of 45 cents

**In 2007
there were**

598

**producer
organizations
in**

59

countries

PEOPLE POWER
Percentage of people
in UK purchasing
at least one
fairtrade product
2007

34%

32%

15%

regularly occasionally never
or rarely

THE MODERN MOVEMENT for fair trade originated in the Netherlands in 1989. It aims to create direct and long-term trading links with producers in developing countries, and to ensure that they receive a guaranteed price for their product, on favourable financial terms.

Many small producers outside the "Fairtrade" system do not receive enough money for their product even to cover their costs, with machinery, fertilizers and pesticides, imported from the industrialized world, becoming ever more expensive.

Coffee was the first product to be traded fairly. Small coffee producers are badly affected by the volatile international coffee market. Those within the Fairtrade movement are able to reduce the number of intermediaries, and sell to traders and processors certified by the Fairtrade Labelling Organization International (FLO), who pay the producers a price that covers the costs of sustainable production.

The retail price of Fairtrade goods may be higher than that for comparable products, but the price paid to the producer includes a "social premium" that provides funds for investment in social and environmental improvements in the producers' community. These include setting up pension funds, employing specialists to advise on reducing adverse effects on the environment, repairing local housing, building roads and funding schools and other educational projects.

The Fairtrade movement also focuses on environmental standards, requiring environmentally sound agricultural practices, including the minimizing of agrochemicals, safe disposal of waste, maintenance of soil fertility and water resources, and avoidance of GM crops. Nearly 85 percent of Fairtrade coffee is organic.

Although the Fairtrade movement now represents retail sales of €1.6 billion worldwide, it still represents only a very tiny percentage of total trade. Clearly there is scope for further expansion.

Samán, Peru

The organic banana producers in this poorly resourced community use the $1-per-box Fairtrade premium to support improvements in their farms, education, water supply and the environment.

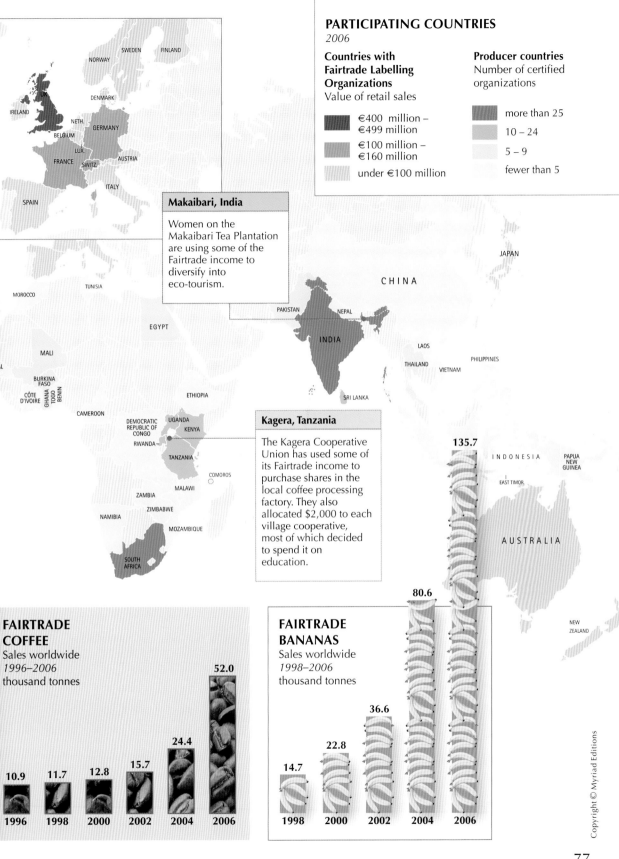

PARTICIPATING COUNTRIES
2006

Countries with Fairtrade Labelling Organizations
Value of retail sales

- €400 million – €499 million
- €100 million – €160 million
- under €100 million

Producer countries
Number of certified organizations

- more than 25
- 10 – 24
- 5 – 9
- fewer than 5

Makaibari, India

Women on the Makaibari Tea Plantation are using some of the Fairtrade income to diversify into eco-tourism.

Kagera, Tanzania

The Kagera Cooperative Union has used some of its Fairtrade income to purchase shares in the local coffee processing factory. They also allocated $2,000 to each village cooperative, most of which decided to spend it on education.

FAIRTRADE COFFEE
Sales worldwide
1996–2006
thousand tonnes

1996	1998	2000	2002	2004	2006
10.9	11.7	12.8	15.7	24.4	52.0

FAIRTRADE BANANAS
Sales worldwide
1998–2006
thousand tonnes

1998	2000	2002	2004	2006
14.7	22.8	36.6	80.6	135.7

PART 4 Processing, Retailing and Consumption

In many parts of the world, patterns of consumption are changing quite rapidly. While traditional staple foods remain a cornerstone of the diets of many people in developing countries, a "nutrition transition", which started in Europe and North America in the mid-20th century, is transforming the eating habits of better-off people in countries such as Brazil, China and India. People are tending to eat an increasing proportion of highly processed foods, which typically contain more dairy products, meat and fat, higher quantities of sugar and other highly refined carbohydrates, and lower levels of dietary fibre, vitamins and minerals. The use of food additives, which aid the production of processed foods and make them more palatable to the consumer, is also growing steadily. This change in diet is leading to increased rates of heart disease, diabetes and other chronic diseases.

Allied to this nutrition transition, and the changing patterns of food production, processing and consumption, a noticeable shift in power has been taking place along the food chain. The influence of farmers is diminishing, while that of large corporations – in particular retailers and fast food chains – is increasing.

Partly in response to concerns about these changes, there has, in recent years, been a marked growth in the demand for, and supply of, organic foods, "wholefoods" and health foods. Overall, food markets seem to be polarizing, with the good getting better and the bad getting junkier.

Ironically, the large corporations that market the highly processed food that is one of the features of the "nutrition transition" have also spotted a potentially lucrative niche market for "nutraceuticals" or "functional foods". These promise beneficial effects, such as better gut motility, or lower blood cholesterol. In short, they are designed to combat the very health problems created by eating a highly processed diet.

30 STAPLE FOODS

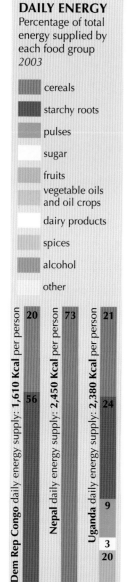

DAILY ENERGY
Percentage of total
energy supplied by
each food group
2003

- cereals
- starchy roots
- pulses
- sugar
- fruits
- vegetable oils and oil crops
- dairy products
- spices
- alcohol
- other

Dem Rep Congo daily energy supply: **1,610 Kcal per person**
20 / 56 / 3 / 12 / 9

Nepal daily energy supply: **2,450 Kcal per person**
73 / 4 / 3 / 5 / 3 / 2 / 10

Uganda daily energy supply: **2,380 Kcal per person**
21 / 24 / 9 / 3 / 20 / 7 / 6 / 10

A STAPLE FOOD is one that is eaten regularly and which provides a large proportion of a population's energy and nutrients. Some form of cereal (rice, maize, wheat, millet, sorghum or rye) is eaten almost everywhere, and in some countries in South-East Asia and northern Africa cereal supplies over 70 percent of dietary energy.

Much of tropical Africa and parts of South America and Oceania are unsuitable for cereal crops, and roots and tubers are the staple foods. The potato is now the most widely grown in this group (and the fourth most important food crop after rice, wheat and maize). The vegetable originated in the Andes, and although its adoption was slow in many countries, it is now grown in both tropical and temperate regions and production is still increasing. It is displacing traditional starchy staples in many countries as part of the nutrition transition, and is used to manufacture a huge range of snacks and other processed foods.

The root crop cassava (also known as manioc) is the staple food of around 500 million people. It can be processed to make many different local foods, such as tapioca, gari, fufu and farinha. It also originated in South America, but is now widely eaten in Sub-Saharan Africa. Yams, cocoyam, taro and sweet potato, are also types of root and tuber.

All these staple foods are good sources of carbohydrate, but contain variable amounts of other nutrients, depending on crop variety and the method of processing and preparation. Cereals can be a good source of some B vitamins, but this is reduced by milling. They also have a higher protein and fat content than roots and tubers, although some root crops contain micronutrients. Staple foods generally need to be supplemented with meat, fish, dairy products, pulses or nuts, to avoid under-nutrition. Dependency on a single crop also creates vulnerability in terms of food security, as demonstrated by the Irish famine of the 19th century.

4 billion people rely on rice, maize or wheat as their staple food

Manioc – a staple food of Sub-Saharan Africa – being cooked in a market.

ROOTS AND TUBERS
As share of total energy supply
2003

- 45% and over
- 30% – 44%
- 15% – 29%
- under 15%
- no data
- 10% – 20% of daily energy intake derived from fruits

Copyright © Myriad Editions

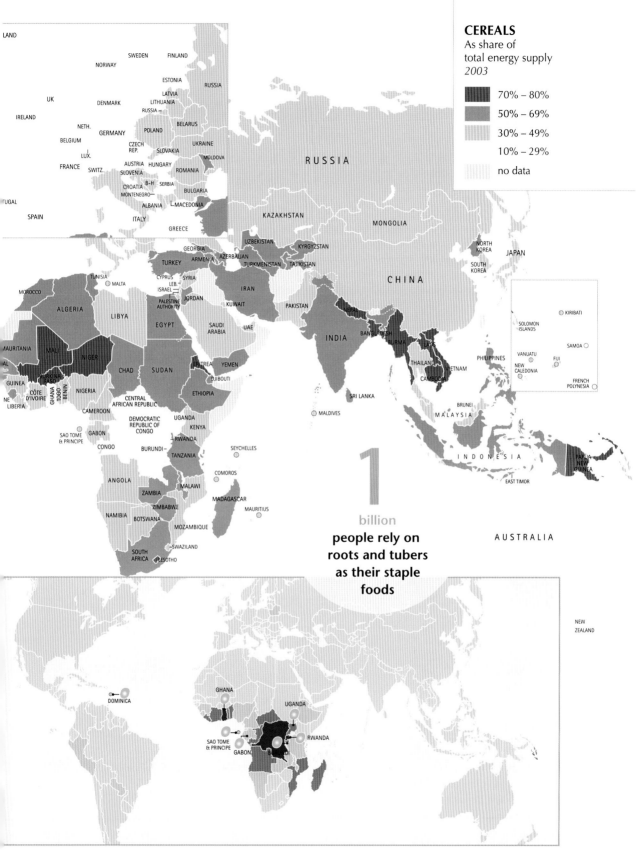

CEREALS

As share of
total energy supply
2003

- 70% – 80%
- 50% – 69%
- 30% – 49%
- 10% – 29%
- no data

1

billion

**people rely on
roots and tubers
as their staple
foods**

DAILY CALORIES

Percentage of total energy supplied by each food group
2003

- vegetable oils
- fruit and vegetables
- cereals
- starchy roots
- sugar, sweeteners
- animal products
- dairy products
- alcohol
- other

Spain daily energy supply: 3,410 Kcal per person

20
7
22

4
10

14

8

5
10

USA daily energy supply: 3,770 Kcal per person

17
3
22

3
18

15

10

4
8

DIETS VARY WIDELY around the world and have evolved over many millennia, largely influenced by environmental factors such as climate and ecology. Social factors are also important, with diet partly dependent on whether a social group is agricultural or migratory. Economic conditions, the development of technologies and opportunities for trade have all played a part in influencing diet. Although many traditional diets in developing countries are dominated by a single staple food, this has long since ceased to be the case in industrialized societies, where the variety of food on offer has never been greater.

Diets in industrialized countries generally contain more food of animal origin and less food of plant origin than diets in developing countries. In terms of nutrients, they contain more protein, more fat (including saturated fat) and more sugar, a higher energy density, and relatively little dietary fibre, carbohydrates and antioxidants. In the USA, for example, only about 20 percent of the total dietary energy supply comes from cereals, with almost as much being supplied by sugar and sweeteners, and by fat. A similar dietary pattern is seen in Canada, western Europe and Australasia. The diet of some southern European countries, such as Spain, differs from this pattern in that it has, historically, contained more fruits and vegetables, and its main fat source is vegetable oil, notably olive oil. This has been called "The Mediterranean diet".

Although a shortage of even staple foods continues to be a problem for sectors of the population in many countries, an expansion in food trade, improvements in global communications, and the penetration of new markets by food corporations, are all having an effect on diet. A "nutrition transition" is affecting urban populations in many developing countries, as well as the previously distinctive national diets of countries such as Brazil and China.

THE NUTRITION TRANSITION

The nutrition transition is characterized by:

- a decline in the consumption of traditional staple foods and other traditional food crops, such as pulses and oilseeds
- an increase in intakes of fat, sugar, salt and often animal foods
- an increase in alcohol consumption in non-Islamic countries
- an increase in the consumption of refined and processed foods
- an overall reduction in dietary diversity

Such changes in diet have an impact on health, leading to an increase in diet-related diseases, such as late-onset diabetes, some cancers and cardiovascular disease.

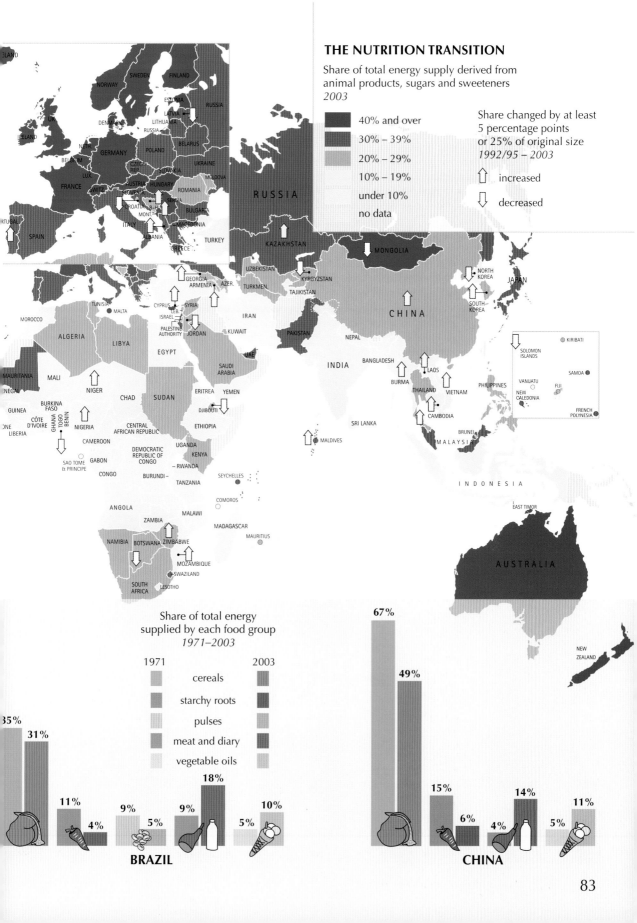

THE NUTRITION TRANSITION

Share of total energy supply derived from
animal products, sugars and sweeteners
2003

- 40% and over
- 30% – 39%
- 20% – 29%
- 10% – 19%
- under 10%
- no data

Share changed by at least
5 percentage points
or 25% of original size
1992/95 – 2003

⇧ increased

⇩ decreased

Share of total energy supplied by each food group
1971–2003

1971   2003

- cereals
- starchy roots
- pulses
- meat and diary
- vegetable oils

BRAZIL

35%   31%

11%   4%

9%   5%

9%   18%

5%   10%

CHINA

67%   49%

15%   6%

4%   14%

5%   11%

90%

of chicken sold in USA is already jointed or processed

PROCESSED FOOD appeals to consumers because it saves time, with the preparation and most of the cooking done in the factory. Food processing is as old as cooking, but during the 19th century specialist companies emerged that took advantage of technological developments and of the economies of scale offered by mass markets. New methods of milling, cooking, preserving and transporting foods revolutionized baking, pie making, dairy products, confectionery and soft drinks. Foods such as white bread, which only the rich had previously been able to afford, were made more widely available following the invention of steel roller mills. Cheap white flour also meant that the processing company could make a lucrative side business selling the bran and wheat germ (rich in nutrients) as animal food.

Processors have often claimed that their products offer health benefits. Coca-Cola, the world's highest-value brand, started as a health product in 1885, as had Kellogg's cereals in 1876. And Henri Nestlé's creation in 1867 of a milk food for infants is claimed to have saved his neighbour's baby's life; today its milk formula is criticized by those claiming it has a detrimental effect in developing countries.

In most countries, a handful of large food-processing companies have emerged, and are concentrating control inexorably. In the USA, alongside the well-known processed-food brand-name companies, there are very powerful meat and raw-commodity processing companies. These control a large share of the market – around 80 percent in the case of beef and soybean, and 60 percent in flour milling. Such processor power reaches back down the food chain, because it applies to every aspect of production. A farmer wishing to supply one of the large processors becomes totally dependent on them, with devastating consequences should the processor decide not to renew the contract.

At the start of the 21st century a two-tier structure is emerging globally in food processing. A number of international giants exist alongside hundreds of thousands of small local or national firms. And as retail power has grown, manufacturers jostle for position, buying each other out or being bought out by private equity firms. They are constantly on the look-out for new brands and for mass, as well as niche, markets.

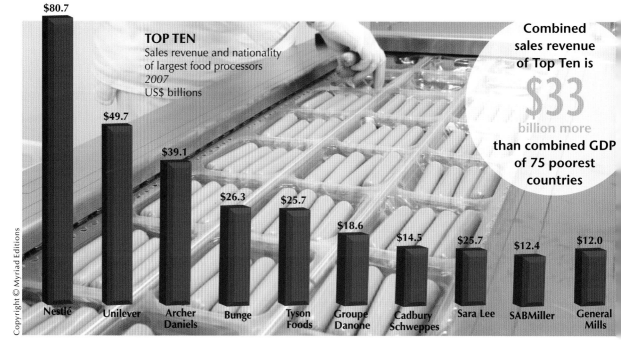

TOP TEN
Sales revenue and nationality
of largest food processors
2007
US$ billions

$80.7 — Nestlé
$49.7 — Unilever
$39.1 — Archer Daniels
$26.3 — Bunge
$25.7 — Tyson Foods
$18.6 — Groupe Danone
$14.5 — Cadbury Schweppes
$25.7 — Sara Lee
$12.4 — SABMiller
$12.0 — General Mills

Combined sales revenue of Top Ten is

$33 billion more

than combined GDP of 75 poorest countries

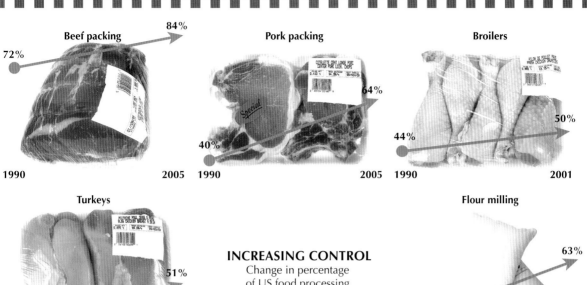

Beef packing
72% — 84%
1990 — 2005

Pork packing
40% — 64%
1990 — 2005

Broilers
44% — 50%
1990 — 2001

Turkeys
31% — 51%
1988 — 2005

INCREASING CONTROL
Change in percentage
of US food processing
controlled by
top four companies
up to 2005 or latest available

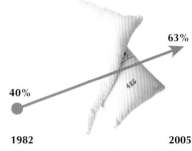

Flour milling
40% — 63%
1982 — 2005

FUNCTIONAL FOODS

Functional foods are marketed as offering health gains and have been increasingly important to the food industry since the mid-1990s. Food, soft drink and drug companies are pouring money into designing and producing what are colloquially known as "nutraceuticals" or "designer foods", aiming for 5 percent of world food sales. Critics say that they do little to resolve the world's nutrition problems.

The bulk of the market is in breakfast cereals – fortified with fibre and sometimes vitamins – dairy drinks and yoghurts with probiotic bacteria, and cholesterol-lowering margarines. However, new products include breads, ready meals, fruit juices and even water fortified with vitamins and minerals.

With huge sales at stake, companies are anxiously steering their regulation and safety regimes through national and international approval systems.

**Global sales
of functional
foods
in 2005:**

$73.5
billion

UK MARKET
Functional food
and beverage products
1998–2007
£ millions

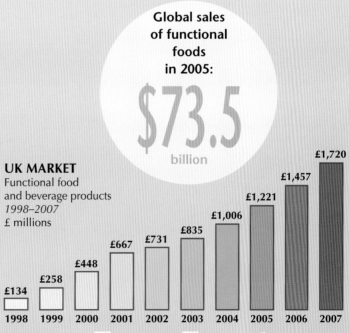

1998	1999	2000	2001	2002	2003	2004	2005	2006	2007
£134	£258	£448	£667	£731	£835	£1,006	£1,221	£1,457	£1,720

33 RETAIL POWER

19%
of global recorded food sales are made by the 10 largest retailers

THE POWER of the food retailers is immense. By a combination of sheer size, tight contracts and specifications, and the application of tough management techniques, they have the farmers – and even giant food processors – dancing to their tune. The retailers use superior control over distribution, and "just-in-time" logistics to drive hard bargains and to reduce their own handling time. Every element in the complex food-supply chain operates in tandem, thereby maximizing efficiency.

A key strategy by which retailers are taking power away from the processors is the use of "own label" or "private label" products – whereby retailers get processors to produce foods exclusively for them, often, but not always, integrating the supermarket's name into the branding. The supermarkets have complete control over these products, from formulation to packaging, and access to the processors' accounts, enabling them to squeeze the processors' profit margins. In Europe, own-label products account for up to 45 percent of food sales. Outside Europe, brand-name products still dominate.

The retail market is highly competitive, with some firms offering a big range, and others the "discounters" – specializing in limited, bu even cheaper, foods. It is also becoming increasingly concentrated. In the UK, seve supermarket chains sell two-thirds of al groceries purchased. In the USA, Wal-Mar accounts for a fifth of grocery sales, but the res of the market is split between a wide range of supermarket brands. In general, the number of outlets is declining in both the UK and th USA, but the revenue generated per squar metre of floor space increased by 9 percen from 2004 to 2007.

Coinciding with rising concerns that foo retailing in western Europe may come unde scrutiny from competition authorities, the bi European food retailers have been increasingl looking towards eastern Europe. Tesc increased its sales there by 75 percent betwee 2004 and 2007. Similar rapid growth by the bi chains is occurring in Latin America and the Fa East.

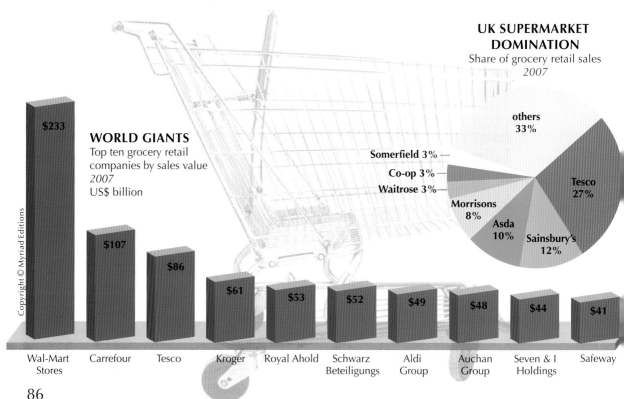

WORLD GIANTS
Top ten grocery retail companies by sales value
2007
US$ billion

- Wal-Mart Stores $233
- Carrefour $107
- Tesco $86
- Kroger $61
- Royal Ahold $53
- Schwarz Beteiligungs $52
- Aldi Group $49
- Auchan Group $48
- Seven & I Holdings $44
- Safeway $41

UK SUPERMARKET DOMINATION
Share of grocery retail sales
2007

- others 33%
- Tesco 27%
- Sainsbury's 12%
- Asda 10%
- Morrisons 8%
- Waitrose 3%
- Co-op 3%
- Somerfield 3%

Copyright © Myriad Editions

EUROPEAN RETAILERS GO EAST

Main European retailers in Asia *2007*

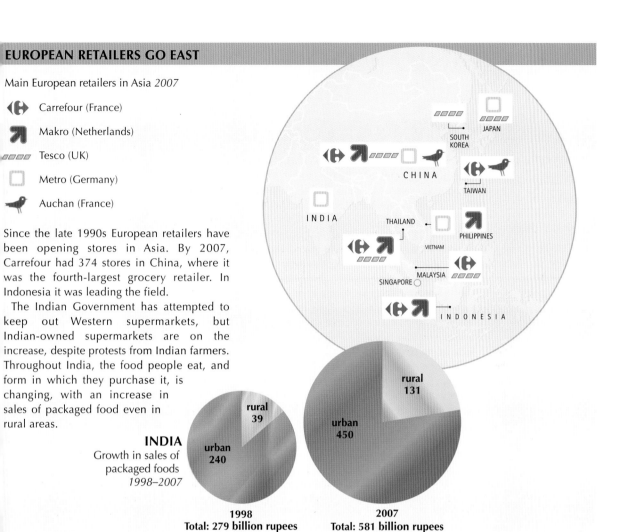

Carrefour (France)

Makro (Netherlands)

Tesco (UK)

Metro (Germany)

Auchan (France)

Since the late 1990s European retailers have been opening stores in Asia. By 2007, Carrefour had 374 stores in China, where it was the fourth-largest grocery retailer. In Indonesia it was leading the field.

The Indian Government has attempted to keep out Western supermarkets, but Indian-owned supermarkets are on the increase, despite protests from Indian farmers. Throughout India, the food people eat, and form in which they purchase it, is changing, with an increase in sales of packaged food even in rural areas.

INDIA
Growth in sales of packaged foods
1998–2007

rural 39

urban 240

1998
Total: 279 billion rupees

rural 131

urban 450

2007
Total: 581 billion rupees

WAL-MART TAKES OVER?

Number of Wal-Mart stores in each country or region
2007

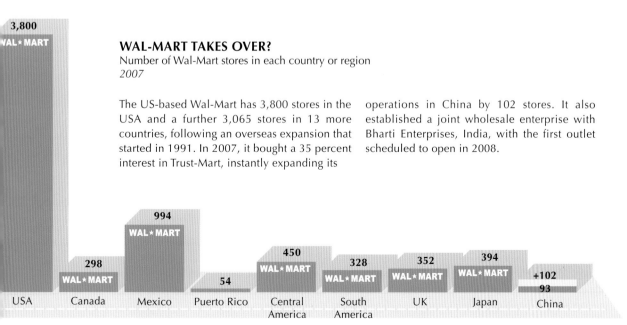

The US-based Wal-Mart has 3,800 stores in the USA and a further 3,065 stores in 13 more countries, following an overseas expansion that started in 1991. In 2007, it bought a 35 percent interest in Trust-Mart, instantly expanding its operations in China by 102 stores. It also established a joint wholesale enterprise with Bharti Enterprises, India, with the first outlet scheduled to open in 2008.

3,800 WAL★MART	298 WAL★MART	994 WAL★MART	54	450 WAL★MART	328 WAL★MART	352 WAL★MART	394 WAL★MART	+102 93
USA	Canada	Mexico	Puerto Rico	Central America	South America	UK	Japan	China

34 ORGANIC FOOD

MARKET GROWTH
World sales
1997–2006
US$

$10bn

1997

$40bn

2006
projected

CONSUMER DEMAND for organic produce is growing steadily. There is an increasing awareness of health and environmental issues, and higher disposable incomes are enabling people to make "lifestyle choices", such as paying more for food they feel will be better for them and less damaging to the environment.

The total world retail market for organic food and drink more than trebled between 1997 and 2005. As yet, it only represents only a small percentage of total retail sales, but average annual growth rates of 16 percent in Europe and 11 percent in the USA are causing excitement among companies eager to tap into this potentially lucrative market. Retailers are promoting organic food more vigorously, and the major food manufacturers are developing organic products to meet the growing demand.

The way in which organic produce is distributed varies between countries, with specialist health-food shops having a larger share of the market in the USA and Germany than in many other countries. This looks set to change, however. In 2005, sales in the mainstream retail establishments in the USA nearly matched those in the specialist shops, with Wal-Mart marketing own-label organic products. And in Germany, discount chains such as Aldi and Lidl considerably increased

their market share, accounting for half of a sales of organic carrots, for example. In the U supermarkets continued their grip on th market, accounting for more tha three-quarters of all sales of organic food ar drink, although in 2006 vegetable-box ar other local-supply schemes grew more tha other sectors.

This suggests something of a return to th original ethos behind organic farming, whic involved the purchase of locally produce food. For although organic production sav energy on the farm (organic milk, for exampl takes 20 percent of the energy input of ordina milk), transporting the food for long distances likely to undo many of its environment benefits. In most countries much of the organ food in supermarkets has been imported – n only tropical and out-of-season produce, b in-season fruit, vegetables and grain for whic demand is too great to be met by nation suppliers. This is the case in the USA, whe much organic produce is imported from Lat America. In the UK, although two-thirds organic meat, salad crops and vegetabl purchased are home-produced, there we signs in 2007 that constraints on the supply home-grown organic produce would curta recent rapid growth in the market.

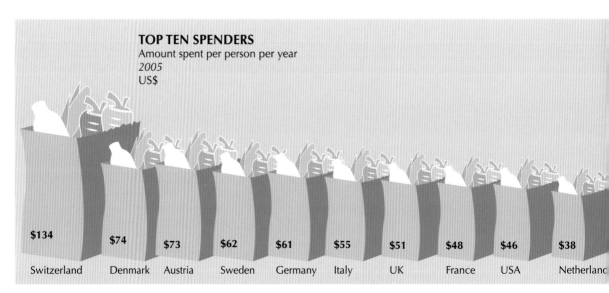

TOP TEN SPENDERS
Amount spent per person per year
2005
US$

Switzerland	Denmark	Austria	Sweden	Germany	Italy	UK	France	USA	Netherland
$134	$74	$73	$62	$61	$55	$51	$48	$46	$38

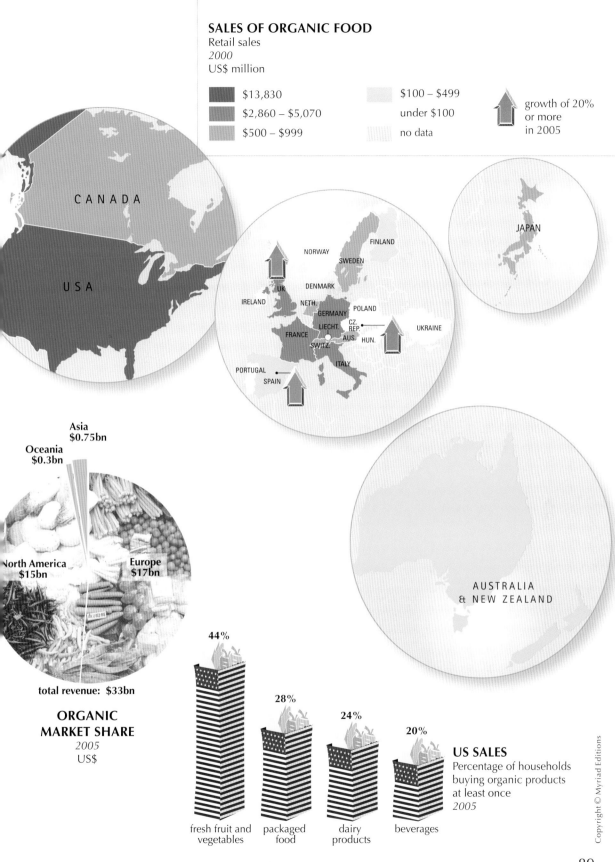

SALES OF ORGANIC FOOD
Retail sales
2000
US$ million

■	$13,830
■	$2,860 – $5,070
■	$500 – $999
■	$100 – $499
■	under $100
▨	no data

↑ growth of 20% or more in 2005

CANADA

USA

NORWAY
FINLAND
SWEDEN
DENMARK
UK
IRELAND
NETH.
GERMANY
POLAND
LIECHT.
CZ. REP.
UKRAINE
FRANCE
AUS. HUN.
SWITZ.
PORTUGAL
ITALY
SPAIN

JAPAN

AUSTRALIA
& NEW ZEALAND

Asia
$0.75bn

Oceania
$0.3bn

North America
$15bn

Europe
$17bn

total revenue: $33bn

ORGANIC
MARKET SHARE
2005
US$

44%
fresh fruit and vegetables

28%
packaged food

24%
dairy products

20%
beverages

US SALES
Percentage of households buying organic products at least once
2005

35 FOOD ADDITIVES

HUMAN SAFETY

540 food additive compounds are deemed safe for human consumption by regulatory bodies, but critics of the testing system have raised doubts about many of them:

320
accepted as reasonably safe

150
doubts and uncertainties raised about their safety

70
may cause allergy and / or acute intolerance in a few people

30
could cause significant long-term harm to any consumers

Dangerous chemicals

THE FOOD INDUSTRY spends over $24 billion a year on chemical food additives to improve the colour, flavour, texture and shelf-life of its products. Consumers in the industrialized countries ingest between 7kg and 8kg (15lb – 18lb) of food additives a year, for which the food industry is paying the equivalent of around $20 per person.

The food industry maintains that it uses additives to protect consumers from bacterial food poisoning and to prevent foods from rapidly deteriorating. But the additives used as preservatives, and those used to inhibit oils and fats from going rancid ("antioxidants"), account for only 5 percent of the total market. Around 75 percent of expenditure on additives by processing companies is for cosmetic purposes – to change the colour, flavour, appearance and texture of a food product. The remaining additives are processing aids such as lubricants and enzymes, used for their effects in the production process rather then on the final product.

The use of food additives is controlled by governments in all industrialized countries and in many developing countries too. For a chemical to be permitted, evidence must be provided that its risk to human health is acceptably slight. As a rule, it is not acceptable to test food additives on humans, and so most tests are conducted using laboratory animals (usually rats and mice), and bacterial and cell cultures. But the results of animal studies are difficult to interpret because it is not known animals or microbes provide suitable mode for humans. The food additives industry ofte treats the results of these studies as valid whe they show no adverse effects, but question their relevance when they do suggest advers effects. Adverse effects that may be blamed c additives include hyperactivity and headache for which scientists have no laboratory te models.

There are many serious and unresolve questions about the safety of many additive and their use is controversial. Recent evidenc that commonly used combinations of additive may together pose greater risks than would b expected has provoked considerable debate i policy and public health circles in Europe, ar caused the European food industry to giv serious consideration to reducing its use c synthetic colourings.

The rules on the labelling of food additive vary considerably between countries, but on common practice is to require labelling of th presence of any additives authorized for us Additives such as colourings, preservatives ar artificial sweeteners are therefore ofte identified on labels, but the identity c flavouring compounds (which are exempt fro the testing and licensing system) are almo never disclosed. Some manufacturers ar retailers are trying to reduce the use c additives, but they are currently untypical c the food industry.

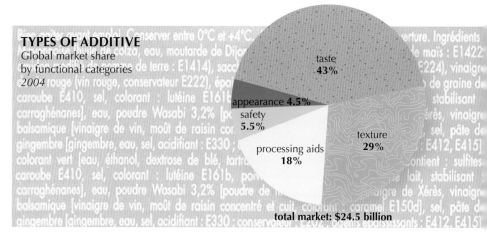

TYPES OF ADDITIVE
Global market share by functional categories 2004

taste **43%**

appearance **4.5%**

safety **5.5%**

processing aids **18%**

texture **29%**

total market: **$24.5 billion**

MAKING PROCESSED FOOD MORE PALATABLE

Many processed products contain similar ingredients – fats, carbohydrates and starches – and their distinctive savoury or sweet character is created by colourings and flavourings.

Colourings Used to modify the colour of the product. 40 compounds (or groups of compounds), of which 18 are synthetic. High levels of colourings are used in cereals, snack foods, dessert mixes, confectionery and beverages.

Preservatives Chemicals added to foods to inhibit the growth of harmful micro-organisms. 50 compounds, of which sulphur dioxide, sulphites, sodium nitrate, sodium nitrite, potassium nitrate, potassium nitrite are the most common.

Antioxidants Added to food products to inhibit oils and fats from going rancid. 17 compounds (or groups of compounds).

Emulsifiers and stabilizers Used to ensure that water and oil remain mixed together. Used in margarine, mayonnaise and baked products. 48 compounds are permitted in the USA and 75 in the EU. Lecithin, a natural ingredient of soybeans is the most common. As the cultivation of genetically modified soybeans increases, so does the proportion of lecithin obtained from GM sources. Stabilizers are added to emulsions to hold them together and to prevent them for separating out. Used in "ready meals" and desserts, emulsifiers contribute to increasing the amount of oils and fat in our diets, and thus to the growing incidence of obesity.

Thickeners Used to thicken a wide range of products, including emulsions. Most widely used: starches. These are modified to control their performance in different types of products. At least 40 different chemical methods are used to modify them.

Anti-caking agents Used to inhibit absorption of water and to prevent powdered mixtures from sticking together.

Sweeteners Excluding sugar, there are 13 widely used sweeteners. Synthetic sweeteners, including acesulfame-K, aspartame, saccharin and sucralose, provide virtually no calories. Nutritive sweeteners such as lactose and glucose syrup are used in even greater quantities. The global market for artificial sweeteners was estimated in 2007 as $3.5 billion. The market leader is aspartame, of which more than $3 billion is sold annually.

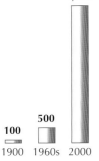

Flavour enhancers Chemicals that trick the taste buds into thinking a food has more flavour. 36 compounds, of which the best-known, MSG (monosodium glutamate), is used in savoury products.

LAVOURINGS
lumber of different
ompounds available
002

4,500

500

100

1900　1960s　2000

Flavouring agents are used to reinforce the flavour of products containing natural foods or to simulate the taste of natural foods in products containing mainly starch and fat. They account for about 25% of industrial expenditure on additives, and over 90% of the compounds. In most countries, flavourings are regulated less strictly than other kinds of food additives. They do not have to be tested for safety and are only controlled or banned if shown to be harmful. One reason given for this is that flavourings are used in small amounts (although this implies that they are powerful and reactive compounds). Another is that there are too many different ones to deal with each one separately. Companies also argue for secrecy on the grounds of commercial confidentiality. Regulators are slowly extending the scope of their controls to include flavourings.

400,000
tonnes
of emulsifiers

650,000
tonnes
of MSG

75,000
tonnes
of sweeteners
are used
each year

INCREASED SPENDING
Total spent each year on eating out
1985–2005
US$ billion

USA

$546
$432
$386
$359
$310

1985 1990 1995 2000 2005

$30 $38 $39 $41 $40

UK

EATING OUT is a global business worth almost $2 trillion, and the USA is a key player. Each year, Americans spend almost $2,500 per person on eating in restaurants, fast food outlets, hotels, schools and at work. In most industrialized countries, annual expenditure on eating out exceeds $250 per person. International trends are clearly apparent in the menus that are on offer, with pizza, burgers and fried chicken becoming widely available in industrialized and developing countries alike. "Fast food", with its casual, informal and relatively quick service, is also becoming available worldwide. However, despite the global reach of the fast-food chains, eating out is a long-established activity in all countries, whether rich or poor, and local culture still influences the style of food on offer in each country. In Italy, for example, the tradition of family-run restaurants means that it is difficult for international players to gain a significant foothold.

Eating out is generally a more expensive option than eating at home, so it tends to be more viable, and therefore more prevalent, in countries with higher levels of disposable income. But there are exceptions at both ends of the economic scale. In the most advanced economies there are many opportunities for eating out at low cost. At the other economic extreme, where many homes may be without a kitchen, there is considerable demand for low-cost cooked food readily available in the street. In South-East and East Asia, the tradition of buying snacks from street traders continues to influence the market: the expenditure on, and frequency of, eating out is especially high in Japan, for example.

CANADA

USA

In the USA the average annual spend per person on eating out is

$2,500

MEXICO

VENEZUELA
COLOMBIA

BRAZIL

CHILE ARGENTINA
URUGUAY

$490,0

RESTAURANT SIZE
Average sales per restaurant
2005
US$

$154,000 — Spain
$163,000 — Italy
$302,000 — Japan
$317,000 — UK
$335,000 — Germany
$354,000 — Netherlands
$364,000 — Belgium
$368,000 — France
USA

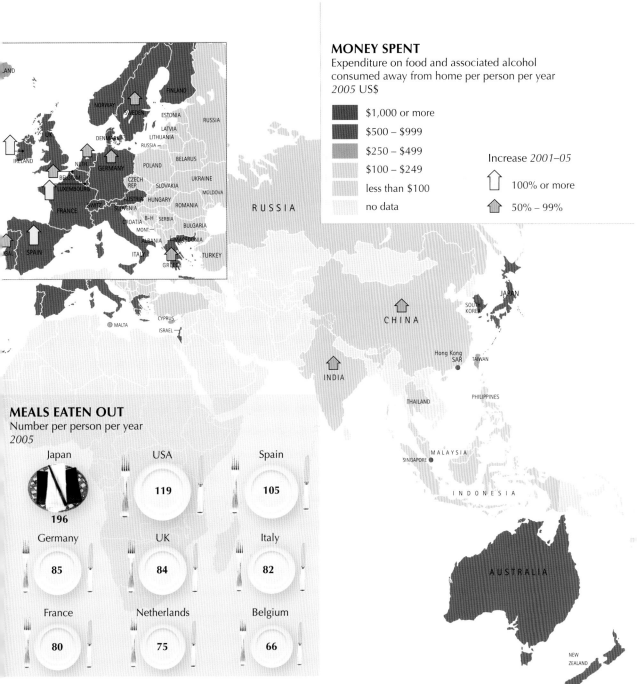

MONEY SPENT

Expenditure on food and associated alcohol consumed away from home per person per year
2005 US$

- $1,000 or more
- $500 – $999
- $250 – $499
- $100 – $249
- less than $100
- no data

Increase *2001–05*

- ⬆ 100% or more
- ⬆ 50% – 99%

MEALS EATEN OUT
Number per person per year
2005

Japan **196**	USA **119**	Spain **105**
Germany **85**	UK **84**	Italy **82**
France **80**	Netherlands **75**	Belgium **66**

Eating out is a growing market. Expenditure in the USA increased by 76 percent between 1985 and 2005, and by 33 percent in the UK. In 2005, almost half of the amount spent on food in the USA was spent on eating away from home. People in other industrialized countries – including France, Germany and the UK – spent about a third of their food budgets on eating out, but the signs are that this will increase to US levels by 2030 or 2035. The increase in eating out in the USA and UK is influenced by factors such as the number of single-parent households and the ratio of younger to older people in the population. It is also directly paralleled by growth in the number of women in paid work.

Although restaurants in the USA have learnt to maximize turnover, average expenditure per person and turnover per outlet vary considerably within Europe, largely for cultural reasons. Many German diners enjoy large, bustling restaurants, whereas in Spain and Italy smaller, family-run businesses are more popular.

In 2007 KFC had over

11,000

restaurants in more than

80

countries

FAST FOOD is a part of all cultures. A meat burger in a bun, a frankfurter sausage, fish and chips, a pizza slice, samosas, deep-fried dumplings, water melon can – all be eaten quickly, out of the home, often with the hands. But it has been the global spread of the three big US fast-food corporations – McDonald's, Burger King and Tricon (Kentucky Fried Chicken and Pizza Hut) – that has come to represent fast food and influenced our eating habits.

Fast food is central to the American way of life. Each day one in four Americans eats fast-food. Elsewhere in the world the figures are lower, but everywhere the trend is upwards. National companies may successfully imitate US style, as with Jollibee in the Philippines, with an annual turnover in 2007 of nearly US$640 million, and 1,589 outlets – three times the number in 2001.

Not all fast food is eaten out of the home, however. Convenience foods, requiring little or no preparation, have become deeply embedded in the food culture of the industrialized world, where the family meal time has been replaced by "grazing" – eating when it is convenient, usually in front of the TV. This sector of food retailing now comprises over a third of the UK market, and is growing at a faster rate than any other.

Fast food and ready meals tend to be high in animal fats. Their popularity has contributed to the rising levels of obesity in the industrialized world – in particular in the USA, where 71 million adults are officially estimated to be obese and a further 50 million are overweight. Fast food does not have to be unhealthy, however. In the wake of scares over the safety of meat in Europe, manufacturers are beginning to respond to consumers' demands for meat-free ready meals. Sales of such products in the UK rose by 6 percent in 2004.

10%

of calories in the US diet come from fast food

NUTRITIONAL CONTENT

Of selected products as proportion of UK recommended female daily intake
2005

- one Big Mac and medium french fries
- one Burger King Whopper and medium french fries
- recommended daily intake

Burger King in North America

Opened 92 new restaurants in USA and Canada in 2007.

Burger King in Latin America

Over 900 restaurants in Central America and Caribbean by the end of 2006, with 34 new restaurants opening in Brazil in 2005 and 2006.

CANADA

USA

MEXICO
BAHAMAS
CUBA
U.S. Navy Base
DOMINICAN REP.
PUERTO RICO
JAMAICA
VIRGIN IS. (US)
GUADELOUPE
GUATEMALA   HONDURAS
EL SALVADOR   NICARAGUA   ARUBA
MARTINIQUE
TRINIDAD & TOBAGO
COSTA RICA
PANAMA   VENEZUELA
COLOMBIA   SURINAME
FRENCH GUIANA
ECUADOR
PERU
BRAZIL
BOLIVIA
PARAGUAY
CHILE   ARGENTINA
URUGUAY

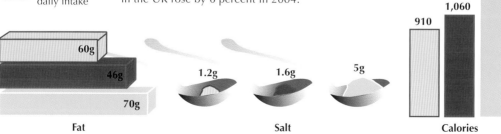

Fat
60g
46g
70g

Salt
1.2g
1.6g
5g

Calories
910
1,060
2,000

In 2007 Burger King had

11,283

restaurants in

69

countries

BURGERIZATION

Number of McDonald's restaurants
end 2006

- 13,774
- 1,000 – 3,830
- 100 – 999
- fewer than 100
- all McDonald's closed down since 2001 for commercial reasons
- no McDonald's restaurants or no data

Burger King expansion

Opened its first restaurants in Poland and Egypt in 2006.

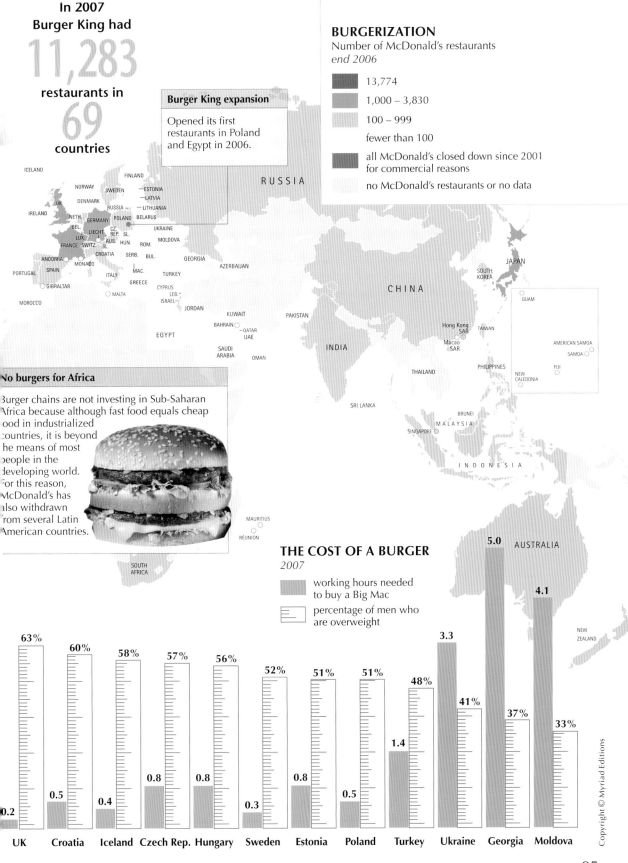

ICELAND
NORWAY
FINLAND
SWEDEN ESTONIA
DENMARK LATVIA
UK RUSSIA LITHUANIA
IRELAND NETH. GERMANY POLAND BELARUS
BEL. CZ. UKRAINE
LUX. LIECHT. REP. SL.
FRANCE SWITZ. AUS. HUN. MOLDOVA
SL. ROM.
ANDORRA CROATIA SERB. GEORGIA
MONACO MAC. BUL. AZERBAIJAN
PORTUGAL SPAIN ITALY TURKEY
GREECE
GIBRALTAR CYPRUS
MALTA LEB.
MOROCCO ISRAEL JORDAN
KUWAIT PAKISTAN
BAHRAIN QATAR
EGYPT UAE
SAUDI OMAN
ARABIA

RUSSIA

CHINA

INDIA

JAPAN
SOUTH
KOREA

HONG KONG SAR TAIWAN
MACAO SAR

GUAM

AMERICAN SAMOA
SAMOA

THAILAND PHILIPPINES
NEW FIJI
CALEDONIA

SRI LANKA
BRUNEI
MALAYSIA
SINGAPORE
INDONESIA

MAURITIUS
RÉUNION

SOUTH
AFRICA

No burgers for Africa

Burger chains are not investing in Sub-Saharan Africa because although fast food equals cheap food in industrialized countries, it is beyond the means of most people in the developing world. For this reason, McDonald's has also withdrawn from several Latin American countries.

THE COST OF A BURGER
2007

- working hours needed to buy a Big Mac
- percentage of men who are overweight

AUSTRALIA

NEW
ZEALAND

	UK	Croatia	Iceland	Czech Rep.	Hungary	Sweden	Estonia	Poland	Turkey	Ukraine	Georgia	Moldova
% overweight	63%	60%	58%	57%	56%	52%	51%	51%	48%	41%	37%	33%
working hours	0.2	0.5	0.4	0.8	0.8	0.3	0.8	0.5	1.4	3.3	5.0	4.1

11%
**of male deaths
in Europe and**

9%

**in the Americas
in 2002
were caused
by
alcohol**

ALCOHOL is not normally thought of as a food, but it is a high source of energy, providing 7 calories per gramme of alcohol, albeit with limited nutritional value. Alcohol is consumed by adults in most countries around the world, although strong restrictions apply in many Muslim countries. Some countries, such as Russia, have experienced high levels of problem drinking, linked to social and economic transition. In many countries, official data do not fully reflect actual consumption because of illicit production and sales.

Alcohol is not a normal commodity. While it does not cause significant problems for many drinkers, and small amounts may be beneficial, it is responsible for some 1.8 million deaths annually – 3.2 percent of all deaths. It also accounts for 4 percent of the world's disease burden – a figure that exceeds that of tobacco. This is largely because the acute consequences of alcohol-use lead to death and disability at a younger age. Many alcohol-related deaths are the result of injuries caused by hazardous and harmful drinking. Nearly a third of

alcohol-attributable deaths worldwide are from unintentional injuries.

Consumption of alcohol in the developing world, in particular of beer, is growing rapidly. In India, for example, the beer market has grown by almost 90 percent since the turn of the century – mostly based on local brands. In Brazil, there has been significant growth in consumption among people on low incomes. In Russia, now experiencing economic growth, people are increasing their consumption of beer, in some cases switching from traditional spirits.

The underlying picture of alcohol consumption is complex, with declines in some areas matched by increases elsewhere, and problem drinking linked to the manner of consumption as well as to volume. The EU is the heaviest-drinking region of the world, and Europeans cause the greatest damage to their health through alcohol consumption, although the average of 11 litres of alcohol consumed per adult each year in 2003 represents an overall reduction of around one-third from the 1970s.

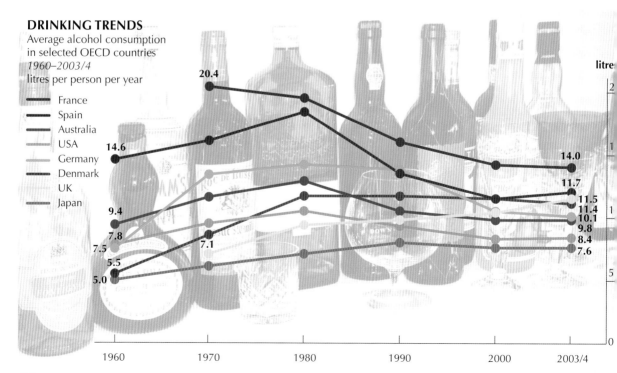

DRINKING TRENDS
Average alcohol consumption
in selected OECD countries
1960–2003/4
litres per person per year

— France
— Spain
— Australia
— USA
— Germany
— Denmark
— UK
— Japan

20.4

14.6

14.0

11.7

11.5
11.4
10.1

9.4

9.8

8.4
7.8
7.6

7.5

7.1

5.5

5.0

litres

1960   1970   1980   1990   2000   2003/4

But while consumption has fallen in France, Spain and other southern European countries, that of northern European countries, mostly notably the UK, Denmark and the Netherlands, has increased markedly. The greatest proportion and level of expenditure on alcohol in Europe is found in Ireland.

In North America there has been fluctuation in consumption, and considerable variation across the region. The number of US teenagers who reported having taken a drink in the past month was 78 percent lower in 1999 than in 1982. By contrast, in Europe some 90 percent of 15- and 16-year-old students had consumed alcohol at some point in their lives – a far higher proportion than in the USA.

The main focus of alcohol control in most developed countries is excise duties, licensing and regulation of advertising, and in the EU, these measures have been explicitly convergent. In the case of young Europeans, there is a risk of alcohol becoming embedded in their culture, in part because of clever marketing and promotions run by the alcohol industry.

ALCOHOL AND LIVER DISEASE
Selected OECD countries
1990 and 2004

average litres of alcohol consumed 1990

number of deaths from liver cirrhosis
per 100,000 people 2004

THE ALCOHOL INDUSTRY

In countries where problem drinking attracts adverse newspaper headlines, the alcohol industry maintains that it has relatively weak influence on consumer drinking behaviour. However, the economics of drinks marketing, in particular the formation of global brands, largely explains recent industry consolidation and the convergence of patterns of alcohol use worldwide

In 1998, the USA was the world's largest beer market, but by 2007 it was China – with Chinese companies emerging among the world's largest. Marketing activities in developing countries occur in an environment with few of the health and safety protections available in developed countries.

The world's biggest brand holder is Britain's Diageo. Formed by the 1997 merger of alcoholic beverage giant Guinness with food and spirits company Grand Metropolitan, Diageo, with sales of $15,761 million in 2007, is twice the size of its nearest competitor, Pernod Ricard. The importance of Diageo – and the alcohol industry generally – to the UK economy is indicated by industry's success in achieving liberalization of alcohol regulation.

Beer sales
1998

35%

10 brewing
groups

Beer sales
2007

35%

4 brewing
groups

**MARKET
DOMINATION**
1998 and 2007

France 11 14 | Germany 14 14 | Spain 10 12 | Denmark 12 11 5 | Ireland 11 5 | Italy 12 11 5 | Australia 11 10 | UK 11 9 | USA 10 8 | Poland 13 8 | Japan 7 5 6 | Sweden 5 | Iceland 5 2 | Norway 5 5

Global advertising budget for food in 2001:

$40
billion

HEALTHY LIFESTYLE CHOICES depend on factors such as price, availability and adequate information about products, as well personal preference and cultural values. The promotional activities undertaken by food and beverage companies can influence all these factors. The global advertising budget for food products in 2001 was estimated to be around $40 billion – more than the national economies of two-thirds of the world's nations.

Several studies have indicated that food advertising and marketing is associated with more favourable attitudes, preferences and behaviours among children towards the advertised products. Even a 30-second exposure to an advertisement can significantly influence the food preferences made by children as young as two years old. Children in the developing world may be especially vulnerable to food promotion because they are less familiar with advertising. They are considered by Western firms as a key "entry point" to new markets because they are more flexible and responsive than their parents, and because they associate Western brands with desirable life-styles.

New forms of advertising are increasingl being employed that bypass parental contro and target children directly. These includ internet promotion (using interactive games free downloads, blogs and chatterbots), SM texting to children's cell phones, produc promotions in schools and pre-schools, an brand advertising in educational material New forms of advertising are occurring i public areas: such as on-screen advertising i public transport and interactive electroni hoardings.

The most frequently advertised foods ar confectionery, sweetened breakfast cereals an meals from fast-food outlets. There is a hug disparity between the proportion c advertisements that promote foods high in fat sugar and salt, and the proportion of our die these foods are supposed to represent. Th intensive marketing of energy-dense nutrient-poor foods undermines health lifestyle choices.

Consumer organizations have called fc stronger regulation of advertising to childre and have voiced concerns that voluntary c self-regulatory controls will not be effective. I

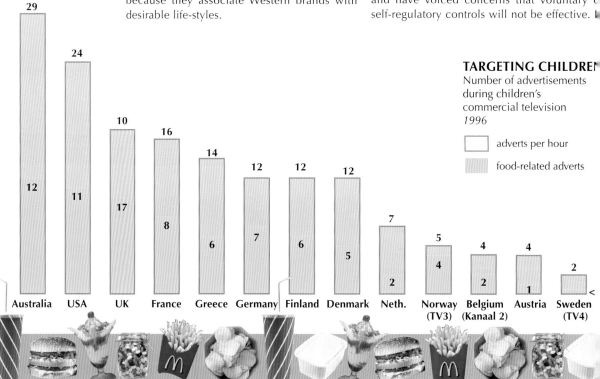

TARGETING CHILDREN
Number of advertisements during children's commercial television
1996

☐ adverts per hour

▨ food-related adverts

7 Over-Nutrition; 31 Changing Diets; 37 Fast Food

DISPROPORTIONATE ADVERTISING

The components of a balanced diet
compared with the time devoted
to advertising them
on children's television
2003

Fatty & sugary foods

Dairy, meat, fish & alternatives

fruits & vegetables

bread, cereals & potatoes

A balanced diet

Fatty & sugary foods

**mainly:
confectionery,
highly sugared breakfast
cereals, ready prepared
foods, and fast-food
restaurant meals**

Imbalanced advertising

response to rising concern among consumers and health professionals, and to its own report on diet and the prevention of chronic disease, the World Health Organization produced a report, endorsed by the World Health Assembly in 2004, that set out a global strategy on diet, physical activity and health. This clearly states that food advertising influences dietary habits, and that messages encouraging unhealthy dietary practices or physical inactivity should therefore be discouraged, with positive health messages encouraged. It urges governments to work to address the marketing of food to children and deal with such issues as sponsorship, promotion and advertising. As of the end of 2008, advertising of junk food has been banned in the UK around children's TV programmes in an attempt to combat an increase in childhood obesity rates.

CATCHING THEM YOUNG

Examples of school-based commercial activities by food companies in the USA

Product sales	• Contracts to sell food and soft drinks on school grounds • Credit awarded for coupons collected by schools or children • Internet sales from which a percentage is given to a school
Direct advertising	• Advertising and product displays in school and on school buses • Corporate logos on school furniture, equipment and books • Advertisements in sports programmes, yearbooks, school newspapers • Advertisements in educational television programmes • Computer-delivered advertisements • Free snack food
Indirect advertising and incentives	• Free educational materials on issues that promote industry goals • Poster contests, reward-based reading schemes • Corporate gifts to schools, with commercial benefit to the donor
Market research	• Student questionnaires or taste tests • Use of the internet to poll students' responses • Tracking students' internet behaviour

40 CITIZENS BITE BACK

FOOD AND WATER are vital ingredients for life. It is little wonder, then, that access to safe, nutritious food has become a political issue worldwide. The production, distribution and retailing of food is, in many countries, controlled by large corporations. Yet, consumers of that food – and the people most closely involved in producing, transporting, serving, selling and inspecting it – have also found a voice, and have formed large umbrella groups that link affiliated organizations around the world.

Many different food issues are the focus of sustained campaigns, which include identifying causes of contamination in food and water, and improving access to safe sources of both, supporting breastfeeding mothers in developing countries, improving animal welfare, highlighting the environmental impacts of unsustainable farming, protecting the health, safety, wages and conditions of food workers, improving food labelling, and counteracting the advertising of unhealthy food and drink.

INTERNATIONAL UNION
Number of unions affiliated to the International Union of Food, Agricultural, Hotel, Restaurant, Catering, Tobacco and Allied Workers' Associations (IUF)
2007

more than 5 | 2 – 4 | 1 | none

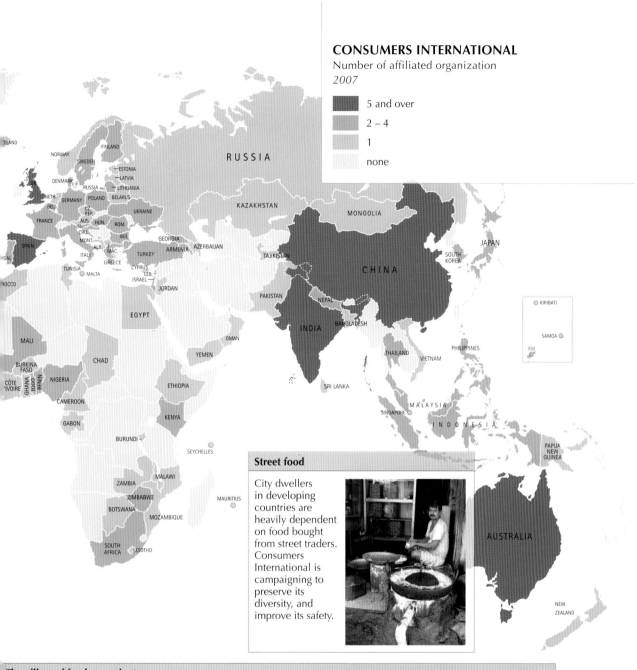

CONSUMERS INTERNATIONAL
Number of affiliated organization
2007

- 5 and over
- 2 – 4
- 1
- none

Street food

City dwellers in developing countries are heavily dependent on food bought from street traders. Consumers International is campaigning to preserve its diversity, and improve its safety.

The pillars of food sovereignty

In 2007, more than 500 people from 80 countries met in Nyéléni, Mali to strengthen the global movement for food sovereignty. They represented family farmers, fisherfolk and urban dwellers, forest, indigenous and landless peoples, and consumer and environmental organizations. They identified six key pillars upon which food sovereignty could be built:

1 Food is primarily a right, not a commodity.

2 The people who produce it should be respected.

3 Food systems should be as localized as possible.

4 Local resources should be controlled by local people.

5 Knowledge and skills should be supported.

6 Nature should be worked with, not against.

PART 5 Data Tables

It is important for citizens, governments, farmers, food industry employees and scholars to have information about the foods that is produced, exported, imported, processed, traded and consumed. It is also helpful to have reliable information about, for example, the environmental impacts of farming and the food system. Information about food also has a more personal meaning in that it helps explain what passes into our bodies daily.

Information about food is astonishing in its range and depth, but it is far from easy for researchers to gather the raw data needed, or to provide accurate estimates. Professional statisticians work long and hard to improve the precision of the figures they publish, but often these are extrapolated from relatively small data sets, or drawn from household surveys and one-to-one interviews.

A great deal of farming, food trade, processing, sale and consumption is not carefully monitored by bureaucrats or statisticians, and figures on the scale of the relevant activities are therefore only approximations. Undoubtedly, some estimates are more reliable than others. The figures provided in the following tables represent those which, in the judgement of the authors, are the most reliable of those in the public domain.

Obtaining access to statistics is sometimes difficult. Too much information remains confidential or only available commercially. In our experience, confidentiality, or the high price charged for access to data, do not guarantee the reliability of these unpublished estimates.

Making information public is essential for good governance. To their credit, governments and academics have made great strides in opening up information, or at least promising to do so. Throughout this book, and in the following tables, we have drawn only on data that have been published or made freely available to us.

Agriculture

Countries	1 LAND AREA 2005 1,000 hectares	2 AGRICULTURAL LAND		3 AGRICULTURAL WORKERS % of total workforce 2010 projected	4 TRACTORS Per 1,000 people 2002
		AREA 2005 1,000 hectares	IRRIGATED LAND % of agricultural area 2003		
Afghanistan	65,209	38,048	7%	64%	0.1
Albania	2,740	1,123	32%	42%	10.6
Algeria	238,174	41,150	1%	21%	36.5
Angola	124,670	57,590	0%	69%	2.4
Antigua and Barbuda	44	14	–	19%	–
Argentina	273,669	129,355	1%	8%	205.2
Armenia	2,820	1,390	21%	10%	94.0
Australia	768,230	445,149	1%	4%	712.7
Austria	8,245	3,263	0%	3%	1,875.0
Azerbaijan	8,266	4,759	31%	23%	31.1
Bahamas	1,001	14	7%	2%	24.0
Bahrain	71	10	40%	0%	–
Bangladesh	13,017	9,011	52%	46%	0.1
Barbados	43	19	26%	3%	–
Belarus	20,748	8,860	2%	9%	95.9
Belgium	3,023	1,386	–	1%	1,377.1
Belize	2,281	152	2%	28%	42.6
Benin	11,062	3,567	0%	44%	0.1
Bhutan	4,700	592	7%	93%	–
Bolivia	108,438	37,768	0%	42%	3.9
Bosnia and Herzegovina	5,120	2,147	0%	2%	341.2
Botswana	56,673	25,980	0%	42%	17.0
Brazil	845,942	263,600	1%	12%	63.6
Brunei	527	25	4%	0%	72.0
Bulgaria	10,864	5,265	11%	4%	125.3
Burkina Faso	27,360	10,900	0%	92%	0.4
Burma	65,755	11,268	17%	67%	0.5
Burundi	2,568	2,326	1%	89%	0.1
Cambodia	17,652	5,356	5%	66%	0.5
Cameroon	46,540	9,160	0%	47%	0.1
Canada	909,351	67,500	1%	2%	1,974.7
Cape Verde	403	74	4%	17%	0.4
Central African Republic	62,300	5,220	0%	63%	0.1
Chad	125,920	49,230	0%	65%	0.1
Chile	74,880	15,245	13%	13%	54.8
China	932,749	556,328	–	61%	1.8
Colombia	110,950	42,557	2%	15%	5.7
Comoros	186	148	–	69%	–
Congo	34,150	10,545	0%	32%	1.2
Congo, Dem. Rep.	226,705	22,800	0%	58%	0.2
Cook Islands	24	6	–	25%	–
Costa Rica	5,106	2,895	4%	15%	21.5
Côte d'Ivoire	31,800	20,300	0%	38%	1.2
Croatia	5,592	2,695	0%	4%	27.5
Cuba	10,982	6,597	13%	11%	103.2
Cyprus	924	165	28%	5%	553.2
Czech Republic	7,726	4,259	1%	6%	213.7
Denmark	4,243	2,589	17%	3%	1,205.9

5 AGROCHEMICALS		6 MEAT PRODUCTION 1,000 tonnes per year				7 FISH	Countries
PESTICIDES g of active ingredient er hectare of cropland atest available 2001	FERTILIZERS kg used per hectare of cropland 2002	CHICKENS	PIGS	CATTLE	SHEEP	Total tonnes caught and farmed 2005	
–	3	–	–	–	–	1,000	Afghanistan
–	61	10	11	41	14	5,275	Albania
0.3	13	253	0	122	185	126,627	Algeria
–	–	9	30	85	1	240,000	Angola
–	–	–	–	–	–	2,999	Antigua and Barbuda
1.9	27	1,156	188	2,980	52	933,902	Argentina
0.1	23	5	10	35	8	1,033	Armenia
–	48	773	389	2,077	626	293,022	Australia
2.1	150	88	514	216	7	2,790	Austria
–	10	35	2	76	44	9,016	Azerbaijan
–	100	–	–	–	–	11,357	Bahamas
1.3	50	–	–	–	–	11,857	Bahrain
0.4	178	114	–	180	3	2,215,957	Bangladesh
27.9	51	14	2	0	0	1,869	Barbados
–	133	145	346	272	1	5,050	Belarus
–	347	484	1,008	265	2	25,767	Belgium
16.5	67	14	1	2	0	14,548	Belize
–	19	16	4	22	3	38,407	Benin
0.1	–	–	–	–	–	300	Bhutan
–	5	168	101	172	18	7,090	Bolivia
–	33	14	10	22	2	9,070	Bosnia and Herzegovina
–	12	9	0	31	2	132	Botswana
1.2	130	8,507	3,140	7,774	76	1,008,066	Brazil
–	–	16	0	3	0	3,108	Brunei
–	49	73	77	23	18	8,579	Bulgaria
0.2	0	31	33	106	16	9,006	Burkina Faso
–	13	561	328	106	5	2,217,466	Burma
0.1	3	6	4	6	1	14,200	Burundi
–	–	17	127	60	–	410,000	Cambodia
0.1	6	30	16	94	16	142,682	Cameroon
–	57	997	1,898	1,391	17	1,235,065	Canada
0.1	5	0	7	0	0	7,742	Cape Verde
–	0	4	14	74	2	15,000	Central African Republic
–	5	5	1	84	14	70,000	Chad
6.7	230	517	468	238	11	5,028,539	Chile
4	383	10,701	52,927	7,173	2,540	49,467,275	China
16.7	313	763	128	792	7	181,072	Colombia
–	4	1	–	1	0	15,070	Comoros
0.1	0	6	2	2	0	58,448	Congo
–	2	11	24	13	3	222,965	Congo, Dem. Rep.
0.3	–	–	–	–	–	3,737	Cook Islands
20.4	674	91	39	81	0	46,378	Costa Rica
–	33	73	12	52	5	55,866	Côte d'Ivoire
2.2	118	31	49	25	3	48,451	Croatia
–	40	31	100	56	7	52,345	Cuba
15.8	154	27	53	4	3	4,249	Cyprus
1.4	120	207	359	80	2	24,697	Czech Republic
1.4	130	166	1,749	129	2	949,625	Denmark

AGRICULTURE

Countries	1 LAND AREA 2005 1,000 hectares	2 AGRICULTURAL LAND		3 AGRICULTURAL WORKERS % of total workforce 2010 projected	4 TRACTORS Per 1,000 people 2002
		AREA 2005 1,000 hectares	IRRIGATED LAND % of agricultural area 2003		
Djibouti	2,318	1,701	0%	74%	0.0
Dominica	75	23	–	21%	–
Dominican Republic	4,838	3,420	7%	11%	3.2
East Timor	1,487	340	–	80%	0.4
Ecuador	27,684	7,552	11%	20%	11.8
Egypt	99,545	3,520	100%	27%	10.6
El Salvador	2,072	1,704	3%	23%	4.4
Equatorial Guinea	2,805	324	–	66%	1.2
Eritrea	10,100	7,607	0%	74%	0.3
Estonia	4,239	834	1%	9%	672.3
Ethiopia	100,000	33,922	1%	78%	0.1
Fiji	1,827	460	1%	35%	53.0
Finland	30,459	2,266	3%	4%	1,492.3
France	55,010	29,569	9%	2%	1,545.2
Gabon	25,767	5,160	0%	26%	7.3
Gambia	1,000	814	0%	76%	0.1
Georgia	6,949	3,006	16%	15%	43.9
Germany	34,877	17,030	3%	2%	1,317.1
Ghana	22,754	14,735	0%	54%	0.6
Greece	12,890	8,359	17%	12%	331.9
Grenada	34	13	–	22%	–
Guatemala	10,843	4,652	3%	40%	2.1
Guinea	24,572	12,570	1%	80%	0.2
Guinea-Bissau	2,812	1,630	2%	80%	0.0
Guyana	19,685	1,740	9%	14%	66.0
Haiti	2,756	1,590	6%	57%	0.1
Honduras	11,189	2,936	3%	23%	6.8
Hungary	8,961	5,864	4%	8%	240.0
Iceland	10,025	2,281	–	6%	838.5
India	297,319	180,180	31%	55%	5.6
Indonesia	181,157	47,800	10%	42%	1.9
Iran	162,855	47,631	12%	22%	37.2
Iraq	43,737	10,010	35%	6%	95.1
Ireland	6,889	4,227	–	7%	974.8
Israel	2,164	517	34%	2%	360.3
Italy	29,411	14,694	18%	3%	1,360.7
Jamaica	1,083	513	0%	17%	11.7
Japan	36,450	4,692	50%	2%	826.4
Jordan	8,824	1,012	7%	8%	30.1
Kazakhstan	269,970	207,598	2%	14%	38.1
Kenya	56,914	27,021	0%	71%	1.0
Kiribati	81	37	–	23%	–
Korea, North	12,041	3,050	50%	23%	19.3
Korea, South	9,873	1,881	46%	5%	95.6
Kuwait	1,782	154	8%	1%	6.6
Kyrgyzstan	19,180	10,745	10%	20%	45.5
Laos	23,080	1,959	9%	75%	0.5
Latvia	6,229	1,734	1%	9%	391.7

5 AGROCHEMICALS		6 MEAT PRODUCTION 1,000 tonnes per year				7 FISH	
PESTICIDES g of active ingredient er hectare of cropland atest available 2001	FERTILIZERS kg used per hectare of cropland 2002	CHICKENS	PIGS	CATTLE	SHEEP	Total tonnes caught and farmed 2005	Countries
–	–	–	–	6	2	260	Djibouti
–	109	0	0	1	0	579	Dominica
4.5	82	297	78	73	1	12,086	Dominican Republic
–	–	–	–	–	–	350	East Timor
2.5	169	209	165	207	11	486,023	Ecuador
–	432	647	2	320	43	889,301	Egypt
–	84	101	14	31	0	43,317	El Salvador
–	–	–	–	–	–	3,500	Equatorial Guinea
0.1	7	–	–	–	–	4,027	Eritrea
0.5	44	13	35	14	1	99,327	Estonia
0.1	15	53	2	350	69	9,450	Ethiopia
–	61	12	4	8	0	40,099	Fiji
0.6	133	98	208	87	1	146,096	Finland
4.5	215	819	2,011	1,473	99	832,793	France
–	1	4	3	1	1	43,941	Gabon
–	3	1	1	3	0	32,000	Gambia
–	36	17	32	47	9	3,072	Georgia
2.3	220	608	4,500	1,167	49	330,353	Germany
0.1	7	30	4	24	10	393,428	Ghana
2.8	149	144	109	72	93	198,946	Greece
–	–	1	0	0	0	2,050	Grenada
0.8	131	176	31	63	1	16,756	Guatemala
0.1	3	5	2	39	5	96,571	Guinea
0.1	8	2	12	5	1	6,200	Guinea-Bissau
–	37	22	1	2	1	53,980	Guyana
–	18	8	37	43	1	8,300	Haiti
2.5	47	141	9	73	0	48,580	Honduras
1.1	109	241	518	42	3	21,270	Hungary
0.9	2,555	6	5	4	9	1,669,287	Iceland
0.3	101	2,000	503	1,334	239	6,318,887	India
–	136	1,333	595	389	52	5,578,369	Indonesia
0.3	83	1,153	–	342	389	527,912	Iran
0.1	111	–	–	–	–	32,970	Iraq
2	499	98	209	572	70	322,582	Ireland
5.7	233	390	18	108	5	26,555	Israel
6.9	173	628	1,559	1,109	59	479,316	Italy
5.8	129	88	6	15	0	18,766	Jamaica
12	291	1,337	1,247	497	0	4,819,116	Japan
1.4	172	116	–	4	4	1,071	Jordan
0.3	3	50	210	366	106	31,589	Kazakhstan
0.3	31	18	11	396	37	149,171	Kenya
–	–	0	1	–	–	34,012	Kiribati
–	99	37	168	21	1	268,700	Korea, North
12.8	415	496	860	224	0	2,075,301	Korea, South
4.6	70	47	–	2	30	5,222	Kuwait
–	21	5	19	91	39	27	Kyrgyzstan
–	7	–	–	–	–	107,800	Laos
0.2	51	21	38	21	0	151,160	Latvia

AGRICULTURE

Countries	1 LAND AREA *2005* 1,000 hectares	2 AGRICULTURAL LAND		3 AGRICULTURAL WORKERS % of total workforce *2010* *projected*	4 TRACTORS Per 1,000 people *2002*
		AREA *2005* 1,000 hectares	IRRIGATED LAND % of agricultural area *2003*		
Lebanon	1,023	388	32%	2%	193.0
Lesotho	3,035	2,334	0%	37%	7.2
Liberia	9,632	2,602	0%	62%	0.4
Libya	175,954	15,585	3%	3%	393.6
Lithuania	6,268	2,837	0%	8%	511.5
Luxembourg	259	129	–	1%	–
Macedonia	2,543	1,242	4%	7%	495.4
Madagascar	58,154	40,843	4%	70%	0.6
Malawi	9,408	4,590	1%	79%	0.3
Malaysia	32,855	7,870	5%	12%	24.1
Maldives	30	14	–	15%	–
Mali	122,019	39,479	1%	75%	0.5
Malta	32	10	18%	1%	–
Marshall Islands	18	14	–	23%	–
Mauritania	103,070	39,762	0%	50%	0.6
Mauritius	203	113	20%	8%	6.3
Mexico	194,395	107,500	6%	16%	38.2
Micronesia, Fed. Sts.	70	31	–	23%	–
Moldova	3,287	2,518	12%	16%	88.0
Mongolia	156,650	130,460	0%	18%	16.3
Montenegro*	10,200	5,590	1%	13%	–
Morocco	44,630	30,395	5%	29%	11.5
Mozambique	78,638	48,630	0%	79%	0.7
Namibia	82,329	38,820	0%	34%	10.1
Nauru	2	–	–	29%	–
Nepal	14,300	4,222	28%	92%	0.4
Netherlands	3,388	1,921	29%	2%	638.9
New Zealand	26,771	17,269	2%	8%	452.4
Nicaragua	12,140	5,326	1%	13%	7.4
Niger	126,670	38,500	0%	85%	0.0
Nigeria	91,077	74,000	0%	25%	2.0
Niue	26	8	–	–	–
Norway	30,428	1,036	12%	3%	1,300.0
Oman	30,950	1,805	7%	28%	0.4
Pakistan	77,088	27,070	73%	42%	12.5
Palau	46	9	–	27%	–
Palestine Authority	602	372	4%	–	–
Panama	7,443	2,230	2%	16%	32.4
Papua New Guinea	45,286	1,065	–	68%	0.6
Paraguay	39,730	24,258	0%	30%	22.6
Peru	128,000	21,310	6%	26%	4.4
Philippines	29,817	12,200	13%	34%	0.9
Poland	30,633	15,906	1%	17%	328.1
Portugal	9,150	3,680	17%	9%	277.5
Puerto Rico	887	223	18%	1%	109.8
Qatar	1,100	71	0%	1%	20.5
Romania	22,998	14,513	21%	9%	114.7
Russia	1,638,139	215,680	2%	8%	83.1

* The data for Serbia and Montenegro predate their separation in 2006.

5 AGROCHEMICALS		6 MEAT PRODUCTION 1,000 tonnes per year				7 FISH	
PESTICIDES kg of active ingredient per hectare of cropland latest available 2001	FERTILIZERS kg used per hectare of cropland 2002	CHICKENS	PIGS	CATTLE	SHEEP	Total tonnes caught and farmed 2005	Countries
5.6	232	136	1	53	15	4,601	Lebanon
–	34	–	–	–	–	46	Lesotho
–	–	9	5	1	1	10,000	Liberia
–	34	113	–	6	27	46,339	Libya
0.2	118	57	106	47	0	141,798	Lithuania
–	–	0	13	17	0	–	Luxembourg
0.8	39	4	9	8	7	1,114	Macedonia
–	3	43	74	147	2	144,900	Madagascar
0.3	84	16	24	16	0	59,595	Malawi
–	683	914	206	21	0	1,390,017	Malaysia
–	–	–	–	–	–	185,980	Maldives
–	9	37	2	101	36	101,008	Mali
11	78	4	8	1	0	2,171	Malta
–	–	–	–	–	–	56,664	Marshall Islands
–	6	–	–	–	–	247,577	Mauritania
17.7	250	36	1	2	0	10,448	Mauritius
–	69	2,411	1,103	1,602	48	1,422,344	Mexico
–	–	0	1	0	–	29,336	Micronesia, Fed. Sts.
–	5	31	48	15	2	5,001	Moldova
–	4	0	0	50	70	366	Mongolia
0.8	91	75	255	83	20	7,022	Montenegro*
–	48	340	1	150	112	934,961	Morocco
–	6	44	13	38	1	43,695	Mozambique
–	0	6	0	36	7	552,745	Namibia
–	–	0	0	–	–	39	Nauru
–	38	16	16	49	3	42,463	Nepal
8	367	635	1,230	355	14	617,383	Netherlands
1	569	149	50	700	500	640,695	New Zealand
2.4	28	84	7	84	0	40,897	Nicaragua
–	0	30	1	47	17	50,058	Niger
–	6	222	210	284	103	579,537	Nigeria
–	–	–	–	–	–	200	Niue
0.6	208	55	116	88	25	3,049,570	Norway
1.2	322	–	–	–	–	150,744	Oman
0.5	137	463	–	486	172	515,095	Pakistan
–	–	–	–	–	–	937	Palau
–	–	–	–	–	–	1,805	Palestine Authority
4.7	52	85	21	56	–	222,756	Panama
–	54	–	–	–	–	250,280	Papua New Guinea
3.4	51	43	105	215	3	23,100	Paraguay
1.2	74	733	103	153	34	9,416,130	Peru
–	127	643	1,467	167	0	2,803,603	Philippines
0.6	116	960	2,092	368	1	192,854	Poland
5.5	126	193	339	105	22	218,242	Portugal
–	–	50	11	10	0	2,968	Puerto Rico
3.2	–	–	–	–	–	13,946	Qatar
0.8	35	266	468	194	54	13,352	Romania
0.2	12	1,534	1,602	1,755	136	3,305,698	Russia

AGRICULTURE

Countries	1 LAND AREA 2005 1,000 hectares	2 AGRICULTURAL LAND		3 AGRICULTURAL WORKERS % of total workforce 2010 projected	4 TRACTORS Per 1,000 people 2002
		AREA 2005 1,000 hectares	IRRIGATED LAND % of agricultural area 2003		
Rwanda	2,467	1,940	1%	89%	0.0
Samoa	283	93	–	28%	4.5
São Tomé and Principe	96	57	18%	58%	–
Saudi Arabia	214,969	173,710	1%	5%	14.6
Senegal	19,253	8,248	2%	70%	0.2
Serbia*	10,200	5,590	1%	13%	–
Seychelles	46	6	–	76%	–
Sierra Leone	7,162	2,880	1%	57%	0.1
Singapore	69	1	–	0%	–
Slovakia	4,810	1,941	8%	7%	86.5
Slovenia	2,014	508	1%	1%	6,760.4
Solomon Islands	2,799	85	–	70%	–
Somalia	62,734	44,376	1%	66%	0.6
South Africa	121,447	99,640	2%	7%	43.6
Spain	49,919	29,030	13%	4%	775.5
Sri Lanka	6,463	2,356	32%	43%	2.7
St. Kitts and Nevis	26	6	–	4%	–
St. Lucia	61	18	15%	22%	–
St. Vincent and Grenadines	39	14	6%	26%	–
Sudan	237,600	136,837	1%	52%	1.5
Suriname	15,600	91	57%	17%	42.9
Swaziland	1,720	1,392	4%	28%	32.6
Sweden	41,033	3,219	4%	2%	1,170.2
Switzerland	4,000	1,525	2%	3%	736.8
Syria	18,378	14,008	10%	24%	66.3
Tajikistan	13,996	4,255	17%	27%	24.4
Tanzania	88,580	34,350	0%	76%	0.5
Thailand	51,089	18,600	27%	49%	10.8
Togo	5,439	3,630	0%	54%	0.1
Tonga	72	30	–	28%	–
Trinidad and Tobago	513	133	3%	7%	55.1
Tunisia	15,536	9,769	4%	21%	36.6
Turkey	76,963	41,223	13%	39%	66.0
Turkmenistan	46,993	33,065	6%	30%	70.8
Tuvalu	3	2	–	20%	–
Uganda	19,710	12,712	0%	75%	0.5
Ukraine	57,938	41,304	5%	10%	118.5
United Arab Emirates	8,360	560	14%	3%	5.4
United Kingdom	24,193	16,956	1%	1%	984.3
United States	916,192	414,778	6%	2%	1,651.8
Uruguay	17,502	14,955	1%	11%	174.6
Uzbekistan	42,540	27,890	16%	21%	56.6
Vanuatu	1,219	147	–	30%	2.3
Venezuela	88,205	21,690	3%	5%	62.2
Vietnam	31,007	9,592	31%	63%	5.8
Yemen	52,797	17,715	3%	40%	2.2
Zambia	74,339	25,739	0%	63%	2.0
Zimbabwe	38,685	15,610	1%	56%	6.7

* The data for Serbia and Montenegro predate their separation in 2006.

5 AGROCHEMICALS		6 MEAT PRODUCTION 1,000 tonnes per year				7 FISH	Countries
PESTICIDES g of active ingredient er hectare of cropland latest available 2001	FERTILIZERS kg used per hectare of cropland 2002	CHICKENS	PIGS	CATTLE	SHEEP	Total tonnes caught and farmed 2005	
0.1	14	2	6	23	1	8,186	Rwanda
0.1	58	0	4	1	–	4,501	Samoa
–	–	1	0	0	0	3,600	São Tomé and Principe
0.7	106	545	–	22	76	74,778	Saudi Arabia
0.1	14	29	10	48	17	405,263	Senegal
0.8	91	75	255	83	20	7,022	Serbia*
2.7	17	1	1	0	–	107,327	Seychelles
–	1	11	2	4	1	145,993	Sierra Leone
–	2,418	76	16	–	–	7,837	Singapore
2.1	–	86	122	21	1	2,648	Slovakia
6.8	416	51	70	46	1	2,759	Slovenia
–	0	0	2	1	–	28,520	Solomon Islands
–	0	–	–	–	–	30,000	Somalia
1.7	65	971	151	804	117	820,750	South Africa
2	167	1,048	3,230	671	227	1,070,730	Spain
0.9	310	79	2	26	0	163,684	Sri Lanka
–	243	–	–	–	–	450	St. Kitts and Nevis
10.3	336	–	–	–	–	1,410	St. Lucia
–	305	–	–	–	–	2,745	St. Vincent and Grenadines
–	4	29	–	340	148	63,600	Sudan
2.6	98	2	1	2	0	40,191	Suriname
–	39	5	1	13	0	70	Swaziland
0.7	100	108	275	135	4	262,239	Sweden
3.6	227	52	244	135	6	2,689	Switzerland
0.6	70	132	–	55	200	16,980	Syria
0.8	30	3	0	25	28	210	Tajikistan
–	2	49	14	246	10	347,811	Tanzania
1.1	107	1,100	700	176	0	3,743,398	Thailand
0.1	7	12	5	6	4	29,267	Togo
–	–	–	–	–	–	1,901	Tonga
–	43	57	2	1	0	13,414	Trinidad and Tobago
0.2	37	101	0	55	55	111,782	Tunisia
1	73	937	0	322	272	545,673	Turkey
–	53	14	0	102	93	15,016	Turkmenistan
–	–	–	–	–	–	2,561	Tuvalu
–	2	44	79	106	6	427,575	Uganda
–	18	523	520	592	9	273,688	Ukraine
–	467	–	–	–	–	90,570	United Arab Emirates
5.8	311	1,331	706	762	331	842,271	United Kingdom
2.3	110	15,945	9,550	11,910	84	5,360,579	United States
3.3	94	45	19	516	19	125,953	Uruguay
–	160	23	18	552	84	5,425	Uzbekistan
–	–	1	3	3	–	151,080	Vanuatu
–	115	739	126	425	3	492,210	Venezuela
2.3	299	322	2,446	181	–	3,367,200	Vietnam
0.8	8	118	–	73	32	263,000	Yemen
0.3	12	41	11	41	1	70,125	Zambia
0.9	34	40	28	97	1	15,452	Zimbabwe

CONSUMPTION

Countries	8 POPULATION		9 WATER		10 CALORIES
	2005 thousands	% annual growth rate 2005	Cubic meters of annual renewable water available per capita 2007	% of population with access to improved source 2004	Average daily supply per person 2001–03
Afghanistan	29,863	3.70%	2,015	–	–
Albania	3,130	0.00%	13,184	96%	2,860
Algeria	32,854	1.50%	423	85%	3,040
Angola	15,941	2.60%	10,909	53%	2,070
Antigua and Barbuda	81	1.60%	619	91%	2,320
Argentina	38,747	1.10%	20,591	96%	2,980
Armenia	3,016	–0.70%	3,511	92%	2,260
Australia	20,155	1.20%	23,911	100%	3,120
Austria	8,189	0.20%	9,455	100%	3,740
Azerbaijan	8,411	0.80%	3,547	77%	2,620
Bahamas	323	1.50%	60	97%	2,710
Bahrain	727	2.20%	155	–	–
Bangladesh	141,822	2.00%	8,232	74%	2,200
Barbados	270	0.30%	295	100%	3,110
Belarus	9,755	–0.50%	6,014	100%	2,960
Belgium	10,419	0.30%	1,751	–	3,640
Belize	270	2.30%	66,268	91%	2,840
Benin	8,439	3.10%	2,765	67%	2,530
Bhutan	2,163	2.20%	42,035	62%	–
Bolivia	9,182	2.10%	65,358	85%	2,220
Bosnia and Herzegovina	3,907	1.30%	9,566	97%	2,710
Botswana	1,765	0.90%	8,215	95%	2,180
Brazil	186,405	1.50%	43,028	90%	3,060
Brunei	374	2.40%	21,795	–	2,850
Bulgaria	7,726	–0.70%	2,797	99%	2,850
Burkina Faso	13,228	3.00%	890	61%	2,460
Burma	50,519	1.30%	20,313	78%	2,900
Burundi	7,548	2.10%	442	79%	1,640
Cambodia	14,071	2.20%	32,526	41%	2,060
Cameroon	16,322	2.10%	16,920	66%	2,270
Canada	32,268	1.00%	88,336	100%	3,590
Cape Verde	507	2.40%	566	80%	3,220
Central African Republic	4,038	1.70%	34,787	75%	1,940
Chad	9,749	3.30%	4,174	42%	2,160
Chile	16,295	1.20%	55,425	95%	2,860
China	1,315,844	0.80%	2,125	77%	2,940
Colombia	45,600	1.70%	45,408	93%	2,580
Comoros	798	2.80%	1,427	86%	1,750
Congo	3,999	3.20%	196,319	58%	2,150
Congo, Dem. Rep.	57,549	2.50%	20,973	46%	1,610
Cook Islands	18	–1.10%	–	–	–
Costa Rica	4,327	2.20%	25,157	97%	2,850
Côte d'Ivoire	18,154	2.10%	4,315	84%	2,630
Croatia	4,551	–0.30%	23,161	100%	2,770
Cuba	11,269	0.40%	3,368	91%	3,190
Cyprus	835	1.30%	913	100%	3,240
Czech Republic	10,220	–0.10%	1,290	100%	3,240
Denmark	5,431	0.40%	1,099	100%	3,450

11 UNDERNOURISHED % of under-fives underweight 1996–2004	12 MEAT		13 OVERNOURISHED		Countries
	Kg of meat consumed per capita 2002	% of grain used for animal feed 2005	% of total energy derived from animal products, sugars and sweeteners 2003	Death rate from coronary heart disease per 100,000 people 2002	
–	–	0%	–	145	Afghanistan
–	38.2	0%	34%	127	Albania
10%	18.3	27%	20%	48	Algeria
31%	19.0	0%	14%	54	Angola
10%	56.0	–	–	72	Antigua and Barbuda
5%	97.6	46%	44%	90	Argentina
–	27.7	26%	27%	277	Armenia
–	–	69%	46%	130	Australia
–	94.1	–	45%	190	Austria
–	15.9	22%	20%	269	Azerbaijan
–	123.6	–	47%	–	Bahamas
9%	70.7	0%	–	40	Bahrain
48%	3.1	0%	6%	90	Bangladesh
6%	88.7	0%	40%	–	Barbados
–	58.6	55%	38%	598	Belarus
–	86.1	–	45%	146	Belgium
6%	74.7	–	38%	61	Belize
23%	16.2	0%	4%	46	Benin
19%	3.0	0%	–	122	Bhutan
8%	50.0	39%	30%	46	Bolivia
–	21.4	63%	23%	135	Bosnia and Herzegovina
13%	27.3	10%	27%	39	Botswana
6%	82.4	58%	40%	79	Brazil
–	56.4	0%	30%	26	Brunei
–	69.4	44%	34%	334	Bulgaria
38%	11.2	4%	7%	47	Burkina Faso
32%	10.7	–	10%	120	Burma
45%	3.5	0%	2%	47	Burundi
45%	13.9	0%	14%	55	Cambodia
18%	14.4	0%	10%	60	Cameroon
–	108.1	73%	43%	138	Canada
14%	26.3	0%	–	44	Cape Verde
24%	28.0	0%	15%	66	Central African Republic
28%	14.3	0%	10%	53	Chad
1%	66.4	51%	38%	58	Chile
8%	52.4	28%	23%	54	China
7%	33.9	36%	35%	72	Colombia
25%	7.6	–	10%	–	Comoros
14%	13.3	0%	11%	43	Congo
31%	4.8	0%	2%	47	Congo, Dem. Rep.
–	–	–	–	60	Cook Islands
5%	40.4	54%	39%	72	Costa Rica
17%	11.3	2%	8%	57	Côte d'Ivoire
–	49.9	71%	32%	263	Croatia
4%	32.2	0%	28%	144	Cuba
–	131.3	–	44%	171	Cyprus
–	77.3	–	39%	253	Czech Republic
–	145.9	–	52%	187	Denmark

113

CONSUMPTION

Countries	8 POPULATION		9 WATER		10 CALORIES
	2005 thousands	% annual growth rate 2005	Cubic meters of annual renewable water available per capita 2007	% of population with access to improved source 2004	Average daily supply per person 2001–03
Djibouti	793	2.70%	366	73%	–
Dominica	79	0.50%	–	97%	2,770
Dominican Republic	8,895	1.50%	2,295	95%	2,290
East Timor	947	1.10%	–	58%	–
Ecuador	13,228	1.50%	31,739	94%	2,710
Egypt	74,033	1.90%	759	98%	3,350
El Salvador	6,881	2.00%	3,546	84%	2,560
Equatorial Guinea	504	2.40%	49,336	43%	–
Eritrea	4,401	3.60%	1,338	60%	1,520
Estonia	1,330	–0.80%	9,696	100%	3,160
Ethiopia	77,431	2.60%	1,355	22%	1,860
Fiji	848	1.00%	33,159	47%	2,960
Finland	5,249	0.30%	20,857	100%	3,150
France	60,496	0.40%	3,343	100%	3,640
Gabon	1,384	2.10%	114,766	88%	2,670
Gambia	1,517	3.10%	5,019	82%	2,280
Georgia	4,474	–1.20%	14,406	82%	2,520
Germany	82,689	0.10%	1,862	100%	3,490
Ghana	22,113	2.20%	2,314	75%	2,650
Greece	11,120	0.40%	6,653	–	3,680
Grenada	103	0.30%	–	95%	–
Guatemala	12,599	2.40%	8,410	95%	2,210
Guinea	9,402	2.30%	23,042	50%	2,420
Guinea-Bissau	1,586	2.90%	18,430	59%	2,070
Guyana	751	0.30%	320,479	83%	2,730
Haiti	8,528	1.40%	1,599	54%	2,090
Honduras	7,205	2.50%	12,755	87%	2,360
Hungary	10,098	–0.20%	10,353	99%	3,500
Iceland	295	1.00%	566,667	100%	3,240
India	1,103,371	1.70%	1,670	86%	2,440
Indonesia	222,781	1.30%	12,441	77%	2,880
Iran	69,515	1.10%	1,931	94%	3,090
Iraq	28,807	2.90%	2,490	–	–
Ireland	4,148	1.40%	12,187	–	3,690
Israel	6,725	2.30%	240	100%	3,680
Italy	58,093	0.10%	3,289	–	3,670
Jamaica	2,651	0.70%	3,520	93%	2,680
Japan	128,085	0.20%	3,351	100%	2,770
Jordan	5,703	2.90%	148	97%	2,680
Kazakhstan	14,825	–0.70%	7,405	86%	2,710
Kenya	34,256	2.30%	839	61%	2,150
Kiribati	99	2.10%	–	–	–
Korea, North	22,488	0.70%	3,403	–	2,160
Korea, South	47,817	0.60%	1,448	92%	3,040
Kuwait	2,687	4.70%	7	–	3,060
Kyrgyzstan	5,264	1.40%	3,821	77%	3,050
Laos	5,924	2.40%	53,859	51%	2,320
Latvia	2,307	–0.80%	15,521	99%	3,020

11 UNDERNOURISHED % of under-fives underweight 1996–2004	12 MEAT		13 OVERNOURISHED		Countries
	Kg of meat consumed per capita *2002*	% of grain used for animal feed *2005*	% of total energy derived from animal products, sugars and sweeteners *2003*	Death rate from coronary heart disease per 100,000 people *2002*	
18%	17.1	0%	24%	105	Djibouti
5%	67.1	–	38%	38	Dominica
5%	37.8	62%	32%	84	Dominican Republic
46%	–	–	12%	86	East Timor
12%	45.0	44%	34%	45	Ecuador
9%	22.5	32%	17%	147	Egypt
10%	21.4	37%	27%	83	El Salvador
19%	–	–	–	65	Equatorial Guinea
40%	–	1%	–	33	Eritrea
–	67.4	–	45%	466	Estonia
47%	7.9	1%	7%	47	Ethiopia
8%	39.1	0%	28%	–	Fiji
–	67.4	–	48%	240	Finland
–	101.1	–	48%	76	France
12%	46.0	0%	18%	77	Gabon
17%	5.2	0%	17%	57	Gambia
–	26.0	35%	29%	503	Georgia
–	82.1	–	43%	210	Germany
22%	9.9	3%	5%	51	Ghana
–	78.7	–	31%	153	Greece
–	97.0	–	41%	–	Grenada
23%	23.8	31%	27%	23	Guatemala
21%	6.5	0%	8%	49	Guinea
25%	13.0	0%	7%	54	Guinea-Bissau
14%	31.8	5%	28%	104	Guyana
17%	15.3	2%	19%	30	Haiti
17%	24.7	44%	30%	67	Honduras
–	100.7	–	45%	296	Hungary
–	84.8	–	57%	145	Iceland
47%	5.2	4%	18%	146	India
28%	8.3	7%	11%	101	Indonesia
11%	23.1	26%	18%	120	Iran
–	–	16%	–	90	Iraq
–	106.3	–	43%	167	Ireland
–	97.1	65%	32%	90	Israel
–	90.4	–	34%	162	Italy
4%	56.8	32%	34%	71	Jamaica
–	43.9	45%	30%	73	Japan
4%	29.8	50%	23%	71	Jordan
–	44.8	45%	35%	336	Kazakhstan
20%	14.3	2%	22%	43	Kenya
–	–	–	28%	–	Kiribati
–	10.8	0%	6%	120	Korea, North
–	48.0	46%	26%	33	Korea, South
10%	60.2	44%	30%	35	Kuwait
–	39.0	38%	23%	214	Kyrgyzstan
40%	15.0	0%	9%	100	Laos
–	45.7	–	37%	426	Latvia

CONSUMPTION

Countries	8 POPULATION		9 WATER		10 CALORIES
	2005 thousands	% annual growth rate 2005	Cubic meters of annual renewable water available per capita 2007	% of population with access to improved source 2004	Average daily supply per person 2001–03
Lebanon	3,577	1.20%	1,206	100%	3,170
Lesotho	1,795	0.60%	1,693	79%	2,630
Liberia	3,283	4.40%	67,207	–	1,940
Libya	5,853	2.00%	99	–	3,330
Lithuania	3,431	–0.60%	7,317	–	3,370
Luxembourg	465	1.40%	6,499	100%	3,710
Macedonia	2,034	0.40%	3,137	–	2,800
Madagascar	18,606	2.90%	17,186	50%	2,040
Malawi	12,884	2.50%	1,285	73%	2,140
Malaysia	25,347	2.20%	22,104	99%	2,870
Maldives	329	2.70%	87	83%	–
Mali	13,518	2.90%	6,981	50%	2,230
Malta	402	0.60%	124	100%	3,530
Marshall Islands	62	2.00%	–	–	–
Mauritania	3,069	2.90%	3,511	53%	2,780
Mauritius	1,245	1.00%	1,744	100%	2,960
Mexico	107,029	1.50%	4,172	97%	3,180
Micronesia, Fed. Sts.	110	0.30%	–	–	–
Moldova	4,206	–0.30%	2,783	92%	2,730
Mongolia	2,646	1.00%	12,837	62%	2,250
Montenegro*	10,503	–0.20%	19,870	–	2,670
Morocco	31,478	1.50%	895	81%	3,070
Mozambique	19,792	2.20%	10,531	43%	2,070
Namibia	2,031	2.10%	8,658	87%	2,260
Nauru	14	2.40%	–	–	–
Nepal	27,133	2.30%	7,447	90%	2,450
Netherlands	16,299	0.50%	5,539	100%	3,440
New Zealand	4,028	1.00%	79,893	–	3,200
Nicaragua	5,487	2.10%	34,416	79%	2,290
Niger	13,957	3.50%	2,257	46%	2,160
Nigeria	131,530	2.40%	2,085	48%	2,700
Niue	1	–2.10%	–	–	–
Norway	4,620	0.60%	81,886	100%	3,480
Oman	2,567	1.70%	369	–	–
Pakistan	157,935	2.30%	1,353	91%	2,340
Palau	20	1.40%	–	–	–
Palestine Authority	3,702	–	203	92%	2,240
Panama	3,232	1.90%	44,266	90%	2,260
Papua New Guinea	5,887	2.30%	131,011	39%	–
Paraguay	6,158	2.50%	52,133	86%	2,530
Peru	27,968	1.60%	66,431	83%	2,570
Philippines	83,054	2.00%	5,577	85%	2,450
Poland	38,530	0.00%	1,601	–	3,370
Portugal	10,495	0.50%	6,485	–	3,750
Puerto Rico	3,944	0.40%	1,776	–	–
Qatar	813	4.50%	62	100%	–
Romania	21,711	–0.40%	9,837	57%	3,520
Russia	143,202	–0.30%	31,764	97%	3,080

* The data for Serbia and Montenegro predate their separation in 2006.

11 UNDERNOURISHED % of under-fives underweight 1996–2004	12 MEAT		13 OVERNOURISHED		Countries
	Kg of meat consumed per capita 2002	% of grain used for animal feed 2005	% of total energy derived from animal products, sugars and sweeteners 2003	Death rate from coronary heart disease per 100,000 people 2002	
3%	63.1	40%	28%	152	Lebanon
18%	15.4	5%	10%	67	Lesotho
–	7.9	0%	6%	45	Liberia
5%	28.6	21%	21%	98	Libya
–	49.5	–	36%	423	Lithuania
–	141.7	–	45%	102	Luxembourg
–	35.4	41%	33%	124	Macedonia
42%	17.6	0%	12%	49	Madagascar
22%	5.1	3%	8%	57	Malawi
11%	50.9	42%	32%	56	Malaysia
30%	16.6	–	36%	–	Maldives
33%	19.0	2%	14%	43	Mali
–	86.9	–	41%	197	Malta
–	–	–	–	–	Marshall Islands
32%	29.9	0%	32%	58	Mauritania
15%	–	0%	28%	168	Mauritius
8%	58.6	49%	34%	51	Mexico
–	–	–	–	59	Micronesia, Fed. Sts.
–	22.7	56%	26%	435	Moldova
13%	108.8	0%	45%	45	Mongolia
–	77.6	70%	47%	224	Montenegro*
9%	20.6	29%	18%	100	Morocco
24%	5.6	1%	7%	43	Mozambique
24%	34.0	–	29%	51	Namibia
–	–	–	–	–	Nauru
48%	10.0	0%	7%	95	Nepal
–	89.3	–	46%	119	Netherlands
–	142.1	39%	50%	160	New Zealand
10%	14.9	32%	27%	50	Nicaragua
40%	11.2	3%	8%	38	Niger
29%	8.6	3%	7%	54	Nigeria
–	–	–	–	–	Niue
–	61.7	68%	45%	197	Norway
24%	49.8	0%	–	64	Oman
38%	12.3	4%	31%	103	Pakistan
–	–	–	–	–	Palau
4%	–	–	26%	–	Palestine Authority
7%	54.5	31%	38%	53	Panama
35%	73.0	0%	–	71	Papua New Guinea
5%	70.3	2%	28%	45	Paraguay
7%	34.5	41%	28%	40	Peru
28%	31.1	23%	26%	58	Philippines
–	78.1	–	39%	200	Poland
–	91.1	–	37%	109	Portugal
–	–	–	–	–	Puerto Rico
6%	90.5	–	–	40	Qatar
–	54.5	57%	29%	271	Romania
–	51.0	49%	35%	494	Russia

CONSUMPTION

Countries	POPULATION		WATER		CALORIES
	2005 thousands	% annual growth rate 2005	Cubic meters of annual renewable water available per capita 2007	% of population with access to improved source 2004	Average daily supply per person 2001–03
Rwanda	9,038	5.20%	551	74%	2,070
Samoa	185	1.00%	–	88%	2,910
São Tomé and Principe	157	2.10%	13,293	79%	2,440
Saudi Arabia	24,573	2.80%	93	–	2,820
Senegal	11,658	2.50%	3,225	76%	2,310
Serbia*	10,503	–0.30%	19,870	–	2,670
Seychelles	81	0.70%	–	88%	2,460
Sierra Leone	5,525	2.90%	27,577	57%	1,930
Singapore	4,326	2.20%	135	100%	–
Slovakia	5,401	0.10%	9,276	100%	2,830
Slovenia	1,967	0.00%	16,219	–	2,970
Solomon Islands	478	2.80%	89,044	70%	2,250
Somalia	8,228	2.70%	1,620	–	–
South Africa	47,432	1.20%	1,048	88%	2,940
Spain	43,064	0.80%	2,557	100%	3,410
Sri Lanka	20,743	0.90%	2,372	79%	2,390
St. Kitts and Nevis	43	0.60%	546	100%	2,700
St. Lucia	161	0.80%	–	98%	2,960
St. Vincent and Grenadines	119	0.50%	–	–	2,580
Sudan	36,233	2.10%	1,707	70%	2,260
Suriname	449	0.80%	268,132	92%	2,660
Swaziland	1,032	0.80%	4,400	62%	2,360
Sweden	9,041	0.20%	19,131	100%	3,160
Switzerland	7,252	0.40%	7,354	100%	3,500
Syria	19,043	2.60%	1,314	93%	3,060
Tajikistan	6,507	1.20%	2,392	59%	1,840
Tanzania	38,329	2.20%	2,291	62%	1,960
Thailand	64,233	1.00%	6,280	99%	2,410
Togo	6,145	3.10%	2,272	52%	2,320
Tonga	102	0.50%	–	100%	–
Trinidad and Tobago	1,305	0.40%	2,925	91%	2,770
Tunisia	10,102	1.20%	442	93%	3,250
Turkey	73,193	1.60%	3,051	96%	3,340
Turkmenistan	4,833	1.40%	4,979	72%	2,750
Tuvalu	10	0.60%	–	–	–
Uganda	28,816	3.30%	2,133	60%	2,380
Ukraine	46,481	–1.00%	3,066	96%	3,030
United Arab Emirates	4,496	6.30%	31	100%	3,220
United Kingdom	59,668	0.30%	2,449	100%	3,440
United States	298,213	1.00%	6,816	100%	3,770
Uruguay	3,463	0.70%	39,612	100%	2,850
Uzbekistan	26,593	1.50%	1,842	82%	2,270
Vanuatu	211	2.10%	–	60%	2,590
Venezuela	26,749	1.90%	44,545	83%	2,350
Vietnam	84,238	1.40%	10,310	85%	2,580
Yemen	20,975	3.30%	184	67%	2,020
Zambia	11,668	2.00%	8,726	58%	1,930
Zimbabwe	13,010	1.00%	1,520	81%	2,010

Column headers numbered: 8 POPULATION, 9 WATER, 10 CALORIES

* The data for Serbia and Montenegro predate their separation in 2006.

11 UNDERNOURISHED % of under-fives underweight 1996–2004	12 MEAT		13 OVERNOURISHED		Countries
	Kg of meat consumed per capita 2002	% of grain used for animal feed 2005	% of total energy derived from animal products, sugars and sweeteners 2003	Death rate from coronary heart disease per 100,000 people 2002	
27%	4.4	8%	3%	42	Rwanda
–	82.6	–	38%	–	Samoa
13%	–	–	11%	–	São Tomé and Principe
14%	44.6	69%	25%	70	Saudi Arabia
23%	17.7	1%	15%	39	Senegal
–	77.6	70%	47%	224	Serbia*
6%	51.1	–	31%	68	Seychelles
27%	6.1	0%	6%	59	Sierra Leone
14%	71.1	10%	–	94	Singapore
–	67.4	–	36%	271	Slovakia
–	88.0	–	37%	141	Slovenia
21%	–	–	10%	46	Solomon Islands
–	–	6%	–	72	Somalia
12%	39.0	35%	24%	60	South Africa
–	118.6	–	38%	110	Spain
29%	6.6	0%	19%	86	Sri Lanka
–	99.3	–	46%	–	St. Kitts and Nevis
14%	124.1	–	39%	48	St. Lucia
–	79.1	–	35%	–	St. Vincent and Grenadines
17%	21.0	4%	29%	87	Sudan
13%	–	0%	31%	92	Suriname
10%	34.2	20%	33%	49	Swaziland
–	76.1	–	49%	227	Sweden
–	72.9	57%	50%	150	Switzerland
7%	21.2	38%	26%	64	Syria
–	8.7	13%	18%	185	Tajikistan
22%	10.0	4%	10%	41	Tanzania
19%	27.9	30%	26%	46	Thailand
25%	8.5	13%	3%	52	Togo
–	–	–	–	–	Tonga
7%	57.8	37%	38%	163	Trinidad and Tobago
4%	25.5	35%	21%	133	Tunisia
4%	19.3	34%	19%	146	Turkey
–	–	13%	24%	243	Turkmenistan
–	–	–	–	–	Tuvalu
23%	11.7	4%	9%	41	Uganda
–	32.3	47%	34%	686	Ukraine
14%	74.4	11%	34%	56	United Arab Emirates
–	79.6	–	42%	204	United Kingdom
–	124.8	60%	46%	177	United States
5%	98.6	17%	39%	117	Uruguay
–	20.7	18%	20%	217	Uzbekistan
20%	32.6	–	19%	–	Vanuatu
4%	56.6	17%	31%	71	Venezuela
28%	28.6	11%	17%	82	Vietnam
46%	14.7	1%	18%	84	Yemen
23%	11.9	4%	12%	39	Zambia
13%	15.2	2%	25%	45	Zimbabwe

Sources

For sources that are available on the internet, in most cases only the root address has been given. To view the source, it is recommended that the reader types the title of the page or document into Google or another search engine.

PART 1: Contemporary Challenges

16 – 17 Current Concerns
Von Braun J. The world food situation: new driving forces and required actions. Key findings. Washington DC: IFPRI; 2007 Dec.
FAO. Food outlook global market analysis. FAO; 2007 Nov. www.fao.org
Sauser B. Ethanol demand threatens food prices. Technology Review. MIT; 2007 Feb 13. www.technologyreview.com
Howden D. Africans unite in calling for immediate moratorium on switch from food to fuel. The Independent; 2008 Feb 16. www.independent.co.uk
USA – maize for biofuels
FAO. Earth Policy Institute 2007. Quoted by von Braun J. op cit. 2007.
US Department of Agriculture figures quoted by Sauser B. op cit. 2007.
Mexico – food riots
Taylor J. How the rising price of corn made Mexicans take to the streets. The Independent; 2007 June 23. http://news.independent.co.uk
Peru – bread price
Bee colony collapse
USDA. National Agricultural Library. Insects, Bees and Entomology. www.usda.gov
USDA. Questions and answers: colony collapse disorder. www.ars.usda.gov/News/docs.htm?docid=15572
Reuters. Asian parasite killing western bees: scientist; 2007 July 18. www.reuters.com
Russia – food price freeze
Russia bids to freeze food prices; 2007 Oct 24. http://news.bbc.co.uk
Food prices freeze extended. News online. RosBusinessConsulting. www.rbcnews.com
Mauritania – rising food prices
Mauritania: high food prices spark protests; 2007 Nov 13. www.irinnews.org
Ghana and Benin – biofuel crops
Tanzania – biofuel crops
Howden D. Africans unite in calling for immediate moratorium on switch from food to fuel. The Independent; 2008 Feb 16. www.independent.co.uk

Kazakhstan – export ban
The Guardian. UN warns of new face of hunger as global prices soar; 2008 Feb 26. p.18. www.guardian.co.uk
Kyrgyzstan – bread price
FAO/GIEWS Global Watch: High cereal prices are hurting vulnerable populations in developing countries. www.reliefweb.int
Yemen – food riots
Yemeni price protests turn violent; 2007 Sept 2. http://english.aljazeera.net
Bangladesh – cyclone
In 2007 a cyclone destroyed a rice crop worth $600 million and the price of rice rose by 70%. http://afp.google.com
China – biofuel crop ban
Times Online. Food price rises force a cut in biofuels; 2007 June 12. www.timesonline.co.uk
China – dairy demand
FAO. Food outlook; 2007 Nov. www.fao.org
China – big freeze
China's big freeze; 2008 Feb 8. http://chinaworker.tk
Australia – drought
Egypt in change of heart over drought-hit Aussie wheat; 2008 Jan 2. www.news.com.au/heraldsun
100 million tonnes...
DECLINING GLOBAL CEREAL STOCKS
FAO. Crop prospects and food situation; 2008(1) Feb. www.fao.org
INCREASING COST OF FOOD IMPORTS
FAO. Food outlook global market analysis Nov 2007. www.fao.org

18 – 19 Feeding the World
FAO. The state of food insecurity in the world 2006. Undernourishment around the world. www.fao.org
World Food Programme. Freeing the world of hunger. www.wfp.org
CALORIES AVAILABLE
FAO. Statistical yearbook 2005-06, Table D.1. www.fao.org
Food aid
FAO. Crop prospects and food situation; 2008(1). Table A4. p.34-35. www.fao.org
A child dies...
FAO. The state of food insecurity in the world 2004, cited by BBC. 'No drop' in world hunger deaths; 2004 Dec 8. http://news.bbc.co.uk
Afghanistan, Bolivia, Tajikistan, Zimbabwe
World Food Programme. www.wfp.org
THE COST OF FOOD
FAO Food security. www.fao.org

UNDERNOURISHED PEOPLE
FAO. The state of food insecurity in the world 2006. Undernourishment around the world. www.fao.org

20 – 21 Unequal Distribution
UN Population Division, World population prospects: the 2006 revision population database. http://esa.un.org
POPULATION AND PRODUCTIVITY
POPULATION
CEREAL PRODUCTION
UN Population Division, op cit.
FAOSTATS. Archive. http://faostat.fao.org/site/395/default.aspx
Kilogrammes of cereal produced...
World Development Indicators online database. Accessed 2007 Nov 29.

22 – 23 Environmental Challenges
International Union of Soil Scientists (IUSS) Bulletin 111. 2007. www.iuss.org
SOIL DEGRADATION
Global environmental outlook 4. Chapter 3. p.93. www.unep.org/geo
RAINFOREST LOSS
FAO. Global forest resources assessment. Accessed via Worldbank Development Indicators online database 2007 Nov 30. www.mongabay.com
IMPACT OF CLIMATE CHANGE
Tubiello F N, Fisher G. Reducing climate change impacts on agriculture: Global and regional effects of mitigation, 2000–2080. Technological Forecasting and Social Change 2007; 74(7):1030-56. Table 8: Range of potential impacts for two climate scenarios (Hadley, CSIRO) and a reference projection of cereal production (A2) for the 2050s to 2080s, assuming agronomic and economic adaptation to climate change. Accessed 2006 in unpublished form.
Proportion of food emergencies...
FAO. Water at a glance. Water & food security. www.fao.org

24 – 25 Water Pressure
CURRENT WATER SHORTAGE
World Resources Institute (WRI) EarthTrends: The Environmental Information Portal. Using data from: Food and Agriculture Organization of the United Nations (FAO) Land and Water Development Division. 2007.
SHORTAGES IN 2050
Population Action International, based on water data from WRI EarthTrends:

The Environmental Information Portal. http://earthtrends.wri.org

IRRIGATED LAND
EarthTrends The Environmental Information Portal. http://earthtrends.wri.org

FUTURE RIVER FLOWS
Met Office and Defra. Climate change, rivers and rainfall: Recent research on climate change science from the Hadley Centre, 2005. Brochure prepared for COP11. Model results are for the new Hadley Centre model, HadGEM1.

Proportion of freshwater...
Amount of water needed...
FAO. Coping with water scarcity. Q&A with FAO Director-General Dr Jacques Diouf. www.fao.org

26 – 27 Nutritional Deficiencies
VITAMIN A DEFICIENCY
Johns Hopkins Bloomberg School of Public Health. Tables on the global burden of Vitamin A deficiency among preschool children and women of reproductive age. www.jhsph.edu/CHN/GlobalVAD.html

West KP. Extent of vitamin A deficiency among preschool children and women of reproductive age. Journal of Nutrition 2002;132:2857S-2866S.

Thanks also to Professor Keith West, Graham Professor of Infant and Child Nutrition, Johns Hopkins School of Hygiene and Public Health for assistance on the provision and interpretation of the data on VAD.

IODINE DEFICIENCY
http://iodinenetwork.net/Score_Card/Score_Card_2006.html

up to 500,000 children become blind...
up to 250 million pre-school children...
WHO. Micronutrient deficiencies. www.who.int

2 billion people are anaemic...
WHO. Turning the tide of malnutrition, Geneva: WHO; 2002. www.who.int

28 – 29 Over-Nutrition
DIABETES
International Diabetes Federation. Diabetes Atlas. www.eatlas.idf.org

CORONARY TRENDS
European Health for All Database. www.euro.who.int/hfadb

HEART ATTACKS
WHO. Global burden of disease estimates 2002. Table 3. www.who.int

OBESITY
WHO. The SuRF Report 2. Surveillance of chronic disease risk factors. WHO: Geneva; 2005.

30 – 31 Contamination
CONSUMING DISEASE
Europe data: WHO Surveillance Programme for Control of Foodborne Infections and Intoxications in Europe.

8th Report. www.bfr.bund.de
North America data: www.panalimentos.org/sirveta/e/index.htm
Africa: cholera cases in 2005. www.who.int/wer/2006/wer8131.pdf
Rest of world: individual country sources.

TIP OF THE ICEBERG
Wheeler et al. Study of infectious intestinal disease in England: rate in the community, presenting to general practice, and reported to national surveillance. BMJ 1999;318:1046-50.

DISEASE AGENTS
www.inppaz.org.ar
Tirado C, Schmidt K. WHO surveillance programme for control of foodborne infections and intoxicants: preliminary results and trends across greater Europe. Journal of Infection 2001;43:80-4.

20% of child deaths
Facts and figures from the World Health Report 2005. www.who.int

PART 2: Farming
34 – 35 Mechanization
All data from: FAO. Production yearbook; various editions.

36 – 37 Industrial Livestock Production
Compassion in World Farming. http://ciwf.co.uk
Henderson M. Beef hormones linked to infertility. 2007 March 28. www.timesonline.co.uk
Harmonization alert 1999;1(6) www.citizen.org/documents/Issue6.pdf

CHICKEN-MEAT PRODUCTION
PIG-MEAT PRODUCTION
PIG-MEAT PRODUCTION INCREASE
FAOSTAT Production data. http://faostat.fao.org

38 – 39 Animal Feed
Flannery T. We're living on corn! New York Review of Books 2007 June 28:26-8.
Global livestock sector development in support of international public goods and the Millennium Development Goals. Powerpoint presentation. Agriculture Department. Animal Production and Health Division. FAO. www.livestocknet.ch/ne_news.htm

GRAIN FED TO ANIMALS
United States Department of Agriculture (USDA) Foreign Agricultural Service (FAS). 2006. Production, Supply & Distribution Online Database. USDA: Washington, D.C. Accessed via EarthTrends database (World Resources Institute). http://earthtrends.wri.org

66% of deforestation...
www.mongabay.com/brazil.html#cattle

40% of wheat grown in the UK...
www.grainchain.com

BEEF PRODUCTION
73% of grain...
FAOSTAT Production data. http://faostat.fao.org

WATER
FAO. Fast facts on water. www.fao.org

10kg of feed
Finishing beef animals for profit. www.kwalternativefeeds.co.uk

40 – 41 Animal Diseases
S.M. Crispin, P.A. Roger, H. O'Hare & S.H. Binns. Rev. sci. tech. Off. int. Epiz., 2002, 21 (3), 675-687 Dr. Le Gall F. Economic and social consequences of animal diseases. http://web.worldbank.org

FAO. Animal disease emergencies: their nature and potential consequences. www.fao.org

Mellon M, et al. Hogging it! Estimates of antimicrobial abuse in livestock. Washington DC: Union of Concerned Scientists; 2001. www.ucsusa.org

Woodhouse MEJ. Food-and-mouth disease in the UK: What should we do next time? Journal of Microbiology 2003;94:126S-30S.

CATTLE, SHEEP AND PIG DISEASES
BIRD DISEASES
Disease timelines in World Animal Health Information (OIE) Database. www.oie.int/wahid-prod/public.php?page=home
OIE Summary of immediate notifications and follow-ups. www.oie.int/wahid-prod/public.php?page=disease_immediate_summary
Update on Highly Pathogenic Avian Influenza in Animals. www.oie.int

Contagious bovinepleuropneumonia causes...
www.fao.org/docrep/004/x2096e/X2096E01.htm

8 times the amount of antibiotics...
Mellon M et al. op cit.

42 – 43 Agricultural R&D
Consultative Group on International Research. www.cgiar.org/who/index.html
CIAT annual report 2006:54. www.ciat.cgiar.org

DEVELOPING RESEARCH
1971 figures: Alston JM. 2006, op cit.
2006 figures: CGIAR Annual Report 2006, op cit. p. 57.

Public–Private split
Agricultural Science and Technology Indicators (ASTI) cited in: Alston JM and Pardey PG. Developing-country perspectives on agricultural R&D: New pressures for self-reliance? In Pardey PG, Alston JM and Piggott RR, editors. Agricultural R&D in the developing world. Too little, too late? Washington DC: International Food Policy Research Institute; 2006.

GM MARKET GROWTH
CropLife International. Global market overview 2005. www.croplife.org
GM TRAITS
James C. Chair ISAAA Board of Directors. Global status of commercialized biotech/GM Crops: 2006. ISAAA Brief 35-2006: Highlights. www.isaaa.org

44 – 45 Genetically Modified Crops
COMMERCIAL CULTIVATION OF GM CROPS
GM CROPS
International Service for the Acquisition of Agribiotech Applications (ISAAA). www.isaaa.org
GM contamination, illegal plantings and negative agricultural side-effects
Genewatch/Greenpeace International. www.gmcontaminationregister.org
GM CROPS WORLDWIDE
James C. Chair ISAAA Board of Directors. Global status of commercialized biotech/GM Crops: 2006. ISAAA Brief 35-2006: Highlights. www.isaaa.org

46 – 47 Pesticides
Pesticides News 68;2005:9
PESTICIDE USE
Per hectare: EarthTrends. The Environmental Information Portal, using FAO data.
Total: FAO database archive. http://faostat.fao.org
The use of plant protection products in the European Union 1992-2003. Eurostat; 2007.
http:// epp.eurostat.ec.europa.eu
Data for India and Japan from: Gupta PK. Pesticide exposure - Indian scene. Toxicology 2004;198(1-3):83-90.
Data for China from: Yang Yang. Pesticides and environmental health trends in China. A China Environmental Health Project Factsheet produced as part of the China Environment Forum's partnership with Western Kentucky University. 2007 Feb 28.
Data for USA from: US Environmental Protection Agency. www.epa.gov:80/oppbead1/pestsales/01pestsales/usage2001.htm
Nicaraguans awarded damages
Nicaraguans awarded $3.2m over pesticides. 2007 Nov 7. www.guardian.co.uk
Over-use in China
China to crack down on banned pesticide use. 2007 August 9. Reuters, cited on www.planetark.com
PESTICIDES
PESTICIDE MARKET GROWTH
PESTICIDE SALES
CropLife International. Global market overview 2005. www.croplife.org
70,000 agricultural workers...

International Labour Organization. World day for safety and health at work 2005: A background paper. Geneva: ILO; 2005.

48 – 49 Fertilizers
Stern N. Stern review: the economics of climate change. Appendix 7g. 2006. www.hm-treasury.gov.uk
www.newscientist.com/data/images/archive/2535/25351501.jpg
www.soilassociation.org
NON-ORGANIC FERTILIZERS
FERTILIZER SHARE
INCREASING USE
FAO. Production yearbook and data files. Downloaded from World Development Indicators database.
10 billion tonnes...
Contribution of animal agriculture to meeting global human food demand. CAST (Council for Agricultural Science and Technology); 1999.

50 – 51 Working the Land
Gow D, Reshaping the landscape: Bigger farms but poor farmers. London: The Guardian; 2000 July 14:28.
ILO. Sustainable agriculture in a globalized economy. Section 4. Geneva: International Labour Organization; 2000. www.ilo.org
ILO. HIV/AIDS and work: Global estimates, impact and response. Geneva: ILO; 2004.
AGRICULTURAL WORKERS
DECLINING IMPORTANCE
INCREASING NUMBERS
FAOStat archive. Downloaded Dec 2007.
IMPACT OF AIDS IN AFRICA
ILO 2004 op cit. Table 3.5.
30% of coffee pickers...
ILO-IPEC. Child labour in commercial agriculture in africa. 1996. Cited on www.globalmarch.org worstformsreport/world/hazardouschildlabour.htm

52 – 53 Land Ownership
Lichtenberg E, Ding C. Land use efficiency, food security, and farmland preservation in China. Land Lines 2006;18(2).
Foley C. Land rights in Angola: poverty and plenty. HPG Working Paper. Humanitarian Policy Group of the Overseas Development Institute: 2007 Nov.
Colchester M. This park is no longer your land. Unesco Courier; 2001 July/Aug. www.unesco.org
Qiang X. China's emerging land rights movement. China Digital Times; 2007 December 22.
http://chinadigitaltimes.net
LIVING ON THE LAND
FAOStat http://faostat.fao.org

15% of the world's...
30% of agricultural land...
Cahill K. Who owns the world? Lecture to the Royal Society of Arts; 2006 June 28. p. 5.
29% of land in the USA...
US Census. http://allcountries.org/uscensus
Brazil – rights for the landless
www.mstbrazil.org
South Africa – land and politics
Walker C. Agrarian change, gender and land reform: a South African case study. UN Research Institute for Social Development; 2002.
India – Janadesh movement
Ramesh R. Poor but defiant, thousands march on Delhi in fight for land rights. The Guardian. 2007 Oct 25. www.guardian.co.uk
Community Self Reliance Centre (CSRC). Land rights campaign monthly update. 2007 Oct. www.landcoalition.org
Australia – aboriginal rights
Bullimore K. The Aboriginal struggle for justice and land rights. GreenLeftonline. 2001 Jan 24. www.greenleft.org.au

54 – 55 Urban Farming
Hong Kong's chicken killers haunted by guilt. 1998 Jan 6. www.cnn.com
FOOD PRODUCTION IN URBAN AND SUBURBAN AREAS
Anh MT, Anh HL, Ali M, Ha TTT. Urban and peri-urban agriculture in hanoi: opportunities and constraints for safe and sustainable food production. 2004. www.avrdc.org
Buechler, D. Adaptations of wastewater-irrigated farming systems: a case study of Hyderabad, India. UA Magazine 2002; 8: 267-72.
www.ruaf.org/node/254
Castro G. Cría de especies animales productivas en zonas urbanas y periurbanas de la ciudad de Montevideo (unpublished). Montevideo, Uruguay; 2002.
City Farmer. City dwellers are growing food in surprising numbers! www.cityfarmer.org
City Farmer. Livestock and urban agriculture. www.cityfarmer.org
Cruz/Medina: Agriculture in the city – a key to sustainability in Havana, Cuba. 2003. www.idrc.ca
Dongus S. Urban vegetable production in Dar es Salaam (Tanzania) – GIS-supported analysis of spatial changes from 1992 to 1999. Freiburg: APT-Reports 12; 2001 July, p. 100–44.
Mekala GD, Buechler S, Peesapaty N. Engendering agricultural research: a case study of Hyderabad City, India; 2004. www.ruaf.org/node/64
Mfoukou-Ntsakala. Agriculture urbaine et subsistance des ménages dans une

zone de post-conflit en Afrique centrale; 2006. www.doaj.org

Moldakov O. The urban farmers of St Petersburg. Urban Agriculture Magazine. Leusden, The Netherlands: Resource Centre for Urban Agriculture (RUAF); 2000 June.

Mougeot L. Urban agriculture: definition, presence, potentials and risks, and policy challenges. Paper submitted for presentation at the International Workshop on Growing Cities, Growing Food – Urban Agriculture on the Policy Agenda, Havana, Cuba. Ottawa, Canada; 1999 Oct.

Mougeot L. Urban food production: evolution, official support and significance (with special reference to Africa). Vancouver, Canada: City Farmer; 1994. www.cityfarmer.org

Moustier P. Urban and peri-urban agriculture in west and central Africa: an overview. Paper prepared for SIUPA stakeholder meeting and strategic workshop, Sub-Saharan region. Nairobi, Kenya; 2000 Nov.

RUAF Fact Sheet. Urban agriculture, food security and nutrition. Urban Agriculture Magazine, Special issue for the World Food Summit. Leusden, The Netherlands: Resource Centre for Urban Agriculture (RUAF); 2001 Nov.

RUAF Partner Cities information on Accra. www.ruaf.org/node/498

RUAF. Cuba – Ciudad de la Habana. In: Urban Agriculture Magazine, Special Issue for the World Food Summit, 2001. Leusden, The Netherlands: Resource Centre for Urban Agriculture (RUAF); 2001 Nov.

Smit J. Urban agriculture, progress and prospect 1975-2005. Ottawa, Canada: Urban Agriculture Network. IDRC; 1996.

Smit J, Ratta A, Nasr J. Urban agriculture: food, jobs and sustainable cities. New York: United Nations Development Program, Publication Series for Habitat II. vol 1; 1996.

Stefanescu/Dumitrascu (2005): From food security to food safety: urban development in Bucharest. In: UA Magazine no. 15. www.ruaf.org/node/775

Stevenson C. Xavery P, Wendeline A. Market production of fruits and vegetables in the peri-urban area of Dar es Salaam. Urban Vegetable Promotion Project, Dar es Salaam, Tanzania (unpublished); 1996.

Tsubota K. Urban/peri-urban agriculture in Asia: lessons from Japanese experience; 2006. www.agnet.org/activities/sw/2006/729863362

The following chapters from Veenhuizen R, editor. Cities farming the future future. RUAF Foundation, IDRC and IIRR; 2006: Danso M. Local economic

development and marketing of urban produced food; Faruqui. Wastewater treatment and reuse for food and water security; Mendes. Urban agriculture and sustainability in Vancouver, Canada; Schiere H, et al. Livestock keeping in urbanised areas, does history repeat itself?; Temple D, Lekane T. Vegetable production in Yaoundé, Cameroon; Tixier P, de Bon H. Urban horticulture. All available at: www.ruaf.org/node/961

The following chapters from Growing cities, growing food – urban agriculture on the policy agenda, Feldafing, Germany: Deutsche Stiftung für internationale Entwicklung (DSE); 2000: Novo MG, Murphy C. Urban agriculture in the city of Havana: A popular response to crisis; Jacobi P, Amend J, Kiango S. Urban Agriculture in Dar es Salaam: Providing an indispensable part of the diet; Potutan J et al. Urban agriculture in Cagayan de Oro: a favourable response of city government and NGOs; Garnett T. Urban agriculture in London: rethinking our food economy; Yoveva A, et al. Sofia: Urban Agriculture in an economy in transition; Mbaye A, Moustier P. Market-oriented urban agricultural production in Dakar; Mbiba B. Urban agriculture in Harare: between suspicion and repression; Foeken D & AM. Mwangi: Increasing food security through urban farming in Nairobi; Torres Lima P. Rodriguez Sanchez LM, Garcia BI. Mexico City: the integration of urban agriculture to contain urban sprawl; Kreinecker P. La Paz: urban agriculture in harsh ecological conditions; Purnomohadi N. Jakarta: urban agriculture as an alternative strategy to face the economic crisis; Yi-Zhang C. and Zhangen Z. Shanghai: trends towards specialised and capital-intensive urban agriculture.

Dar-es-Salaam, Tanzania
Dongus S. op cit.
Stevenson C et al. op cit.
Caracas, Venezuela
FAO. www.fao.org/newsroom/en/field/2004/37627/index.html
London
Garnett, T. in Growing cities, growing food. op. cit.
URBANIZATION
UN Population Division.

56 – 57 Fishing and Aquaculture
FAO. The state of world fisheries and aquaculture 2006, Rome: FAO; 2006. www.fao.org
Marine Conservation Society. www.mcsuk.org/mcsaction/fisheries/fish+farming
FISH PRODUCTION
FAO Fisheries Technical Paper 457.

Review of the state of world marine fishery resources. Csirke J. Global production and state of marine fishery resources. Fig. A2.2 Percentage of stocks exploited beyond MSY levels (O+D+R), at MSY levels (F), and below MSY levels (U+M) by FAO statistical areas in 2004. www.fao.org
FAO. World fisheries production by capture and aquaculture 2005. www.fao.org
WHERE FISH COMES FROM WHERE IT GOES
STATE OF FISH STOCKS
CHANGING BALANCE
Fish consumption in wealthy countries...
FAO. The state of world fisheries and aquaculture 2006, Rome: FAO; 2006. www.fao.org

58 – 59 Agricultural Biodiversity
FAO sounds alarm on loss of livestock breeds. FAO Newsroom 2007 Sept 4. www.fao.org
GENETIC ORIGINS
Rissler J, Mellon M. The ecological risks of engineered crops. London, England and Cambridge, Mass: The MIT Press; 1996. Map based on research by Professor Jack R Harlan, University of Illinois, cited in National Geographic; 1991 April.
VEGETABLES AND FRUIT
CHINA
Rissler & Mellon op cit
ENDANGERED DOMESTIC BREEDS
Commission on Genetic Resources for Food and Agriculture. The state of the world's animal genetic resources for food and agriculture. Rome: FAO; 2007. p. 73-74.

60 – 61 Organic Farming
Parrott N, Marsden T. The real green revolution. London: Greenpeace Environmental Trust; 2002. www.organic-europe.net
Willer H and Yussefi M, editors. The world of organic agriculture. Statistics and emerging trends 2007. Bonn, Germany: IFOAM and Frick, Switzerland: FiBL; 2007. www.ifoam.org

ORGANIC FARMING
Willer & Yussefi, op cit. Annex tables.
INCREASE IN ORGANIC LAND
Willer H. Statistics, support schemes and research. In: Willer & Yussefi. op cit.
Haumann B. Organic farming in North America. In: Willer & Yussefi, op cit.
AREA CERTIFIED ORGANIC
Willer & Yussefi, op cit.
INCREASE IN LIVESTOCK
Haumann B. Willer & Yussefi. op. cit.

62 – 63 Greenhouse Gases
Bellarby J, Foereid B, Hastings A, Smith P. Cool farming: climate impacts of agriculture and mitigation potential. London: Greenpeace. 2008.
GREENHOUSE GAS EMISSIONS
GLOBAL WARMING POTENTIAL
WORLD AGRICULTURAL EMISSIONS
Bellarby et al. op cit.
FROM FARM GATE TO PLATE
Sustain, quoted in Holt D, Watson A. The Dilemma of flower miles – examining the trade-off between local sourcing and Fairtrade purchases. Working Paper for the Business and Sustainability Conference, Portland; 2007 Nov. www.walmartfacts.com
COMPARATIVE EMISSIONS
Dijkstra WJ and Dings JMW. Specific energy consumption and emissions of freight transport. Centre for energy conservation and environmental technology. Delft: The Netherlands; 1997.
Gavin A, Marine Director, Lloyd's Register. Shipping faces call for carbon pricing; 2006 Oct. www.maritime-union.org
UK FOOD-RELATED GREENHOUSE GAS CONSUMPTION
Garnett T: Food and climate change. food on a plate. Powerpoint presentation on Food Climate Research Network. www.fcrn.org.uk
Shopping by car
Smith A, et al. The validity of food miles as an indicator of sustainable development. Produced for Defra by AEA Technology Environment; 2005 July. http://statistics.defra.gov.uk

PART 3: Trade
66 – 67 Trade Flows
All data: World Trade Organization. www.wto.org

68 – 69 Live Animal Transport
LIVE TRANSPORT AROUND THE WORLD
LIVE TRANSPORT IN EUROPE
Peter Stevenson, Compassion in World Farming. ciwf.org.uk
43 million animals...
FAOSTAT Archive. www.fao.org

70 – 71 Subsidized Trade
Oxfam. Rigged rules and double standards. Oxford: Oxfam. 2000.
SUPPORT TO PRODUCERS
FLUCTUATING SUBSIDIES
SHARE OF SUBSIDY
MARKET PRICE SUPPORT
Agricultural Policies in OECD countries. OECD. 2007. http://dx.doi.org/10.1787/073451103830
TOP TEN RECIPIENTS
Farm Subsidy Database. http://farm.ewg.org/farm

72 – 73 Trade Disputes
MOST COMBATIVE COUNTRIES
World Trade Organization Disputes. www.wto.org
THE BANANA DISPUTE
World Trade Organization. www.wto.org
Food and Agriculture Organization Commodities and Trade. Bananas. www.fao.org
EXPORT SHARE
BananaLink. www.bananalink.org.uk
IMPORT SHARE
FAO. Banana Statistics 2005. www.fao.org/es/ESC/en/15/190/index.html
BANANA EXPORTERS
FAO. Banana Notes. www.bananalink.org.uk

74 – 75 Trade Dependency
World Bank. World Development Report 2008. Washington DC: World Bank; 2007.
Oxfam. Trade briefing paper. Oxford: Oxfam. 2004.
AGRICULTURE'S ECONOMIC SIGNIFICANCE
World Development Indicators online.
PRICE FLUCTUATION
Fairtrade Foundation, London. www.fairtrade.org.uk
FOOD TRADED INTERNATIONALLY
Regmi A, Gehlhar M. New directions in global food markets. Agriculture Information Bulletin (AIB794) 81. Washington DC: USDA ERS; 2005.

76 – 77 Fair Trade
Fairtrade Labelling Organizations International (FLO). www.fairtrade.net
PARTICIPATING COUNTRIES
Shaping global partnerships. FLO Annual Report 2006/07. www.fairtrade.net
FAIRTRADE COFFEE
FAIRTRADE BANANAS
FLO Annual Reports 2003/4; 2004/5; 2005/6; 2006/7.
PEOPLE POWER
TNS Omnimas, Topline Results; 2007 April. Courtesy Fairtrade Foundation, London.

PART 4: Processing, Retailing and Consumption
80 – 81 Staple Foods
All data: FAO database, Food Security. www.fao.org
ROOTS AND TUBERS
Additional source for Papua New Guinea: Bourke M. Sweet potato in Papua New Guinea. http://rspas.anu.edu.au

82 – 83 Changing Diets
All data: FAO database, Food Security. www.fao.org

84 – 85 Processing Giants
TOP TEN
Combined sales revenue...
Forbes Global 2000. http://forbes.com
World Development Indicators online database.
INCREASING CONTROL
Hendrickson M, Heffernan W. Concentration of agricultural markets. Department of Rural Sociology, University of Missouri. 2007 April. www.nfu.org/wp-content/2007-heffernanreport.pdf
FUNCTIONAL FOODS
Lang T. BMJ editorial: functional foods. British Medical Journal 2007;334:1015-6.
Pharma Business Daily. Functional foods. www.pharmsinfo.com
UK MARKET
IGD. Food and groceries insight & best practice. www.igd.com
Global sales...
Just-food. Global market review of functional foods. www.just-food.com/store/product.aspx?ID=44028

86 – 87 Retail Power
Euromonitor International 2007 report, cited in Barling D, Lang T and Rayner M. Report to Future Look project (EU); 2007 Oct.
UK SUPERMARKET DOMINATION
WORLD GIANTS
INDIA
Annual revenue...
19% of all global...
Euromonitor International 2008.
EUROPEAN RETAILERS GO EAST
www.carrefour.com
www.tescocorporate.com
www.makroasia.com
www.metrogroup.de
www.groupe-auchan.com
WAL-MART TAKES OVER
Wal-Mart Annual Report 2007. http://walmartstores.com

88 – 89 Organic Food
Willer H and Yussefi M, editors. The world of organic agriculture. Statistics and emerging trends 2007. Bonn, Germany: IFOAM and Frick, Switzerland: FiBL; 2007. www.ifoam.org
Organic food sales hit £2bn in UK. BBC News item. 2007 Aug 31. http://news.bbc.co.uk
MARKET GROWTH
Sahota A. Overview of the global market of organic food and drink. In: Willer & Yussefi. 2007 op cit.
TOP TEN SPENDERS
SALES OF ORGANIC FOOD
ORGANIC MARKET SHARE
Sahota A. op cit.
Richter T. and Padel S. The European market for organic food. In: Willer & Yussefi M. 2007 op cit.

Haumann B. Organic farming in North America. In: Willer & Yussefi M. 2007 op cit.

US SALES
Haumann B. op .cit.

90 – 91 Food Additives
BCC Research. The global market for flavors and fragrances; 2006 Dec. www.bccresearch.com
Frost & Sullivan. Global market review of food and drink additives - Forecasts to 2012; 2007 Jan.
Frost & Sullivan, US and Europe food additives and preservatives – investment analysis; 2007 Nov.
Global Industry Analysts. Artificial sweeteners: a global strategic business report; 2007 July.
Leatherhead Food International, The food additives market: global trends and developments. 3rd edition; 2005 June.

TYPES OF ADDITIVE
Leatherhead Food International, op cit.

92 – 93 Eating Out
All data: Horizons FS Limited. www.horizonsforsuccess.com

94 – 95 Fast Food
Healthy fast food: guide to healthy fast food eating. www.helpguide.org/life/fast_food_nutrition.htm
Jollibee Foods Corporation. Consolidated statement of income for the period ended September 2007 www.jollibee.com
The Grocer. Ready meals a third of take home foods: 2004 April. www.thegrocer.co.uk
Obesity trends. www.obesityinamerica.org/trends.html
Clinical guidelines on the identification, evaluation and treatment of overweight and obesity in adults. www.nhlbi.nih.gov
Market Assessments Publications Ltd. Vegetarian foods; 2004 Sept. www.pharmsinfo.com

BURGERIZATION
www.mcdonalds.com
In 2007 Burger King...
www.allhailtheking.bk.com
In 2007 KFC...
www.kfc.com/about/default.asp
THE COST OF A BURGER
IOTF 2007
Lobstein T, Jackson Leach R. Obesity – international comparisons. Submission to the UK Government Foresight study: Tackling obesities: future choices. Data derived from the Big Mac index published annually in The Economist, the ILO website for average hourly rates of pay, and the IOTF for prevalence data for adult male overweight. www.foresight.gov.uk/Obesity/Obesity.html

NUTRITIONAL CONTENT
10% of calories...
Hurley J and Liebman B. Fast food in '05. Nutrition Action Healthletter; 2005 Mar. Center for Science in the Public Interest. www.cspinet.org

96 – 97 Alcohol
Canadean. www.canadean.com
Key Note Ltd. www.keynote.co.uk
Institute for Alcohol Studies. www.ias.org.uk
DRINKING TRENDS
OECD Health data 2006. www.oecd.org
EFFECT ON HEALTH
OECD Health at a glance 2007. www.oecd.org
11% of male deaths...
World Health Organization.

98 – 99 Advertising and Marketing
Borzekowski DL, Robinson TN. The 30-second effect: an experiment revealing the impact of television commercials on food preferences of preschoolers. Journal of the American Dietetic Association 2001;101:42-6.
Food Commission. What retailers say… and what manufacturers say. Food Magazine 63; 2003Oct.
Hastings G, McDermott L, Angus K, Stead M, Thomson S. The extent, nature and effects of food promotion to children: a review of the evidence. Background document 1, WHO forum and technical meeting on the marketing of food and non-alcoholic beverages to children, Lysebu (Oslo), Norway; 2006 May.
Dalmeny K, Hanna E, Lobstein T, editors. Broadcasting bad health. London: International Association of Consumer Food Organizations; 2003. www.foodcomm.org.uk
Taras HL, Sallis JF, Patterson TL, Nader PR, Nelson JA. Television's influence on children's diet. 1989.
Coon KA, Tucker KL. Television and children's consumption patterns: a review of the literature. Minerva Pediatr 2002;54:423-36.
World Health Organization. Report of a Joint WHO/FAO Expert Consultation. Diet, nutrition and the prevention of chronic diseases. WHO Technical Report Series 916. Geneva: WHO; 2002.
World Health Organization: Global strategy on diet, physical activity and health. Geneva: WHO; 2004.
TARGETING CHILDREN
Dibb S; 1996.
DISPROPORTIONATE ADVERTISING
Dalmeny K. Food Commission. First published in Broadcasting bad health. www.foodcomm.org.uk/press_junk_marketing_03.htm

100 – 101 Citizens Bite Back
CONSUMERS INTERNATIONAL
www.consumersinternational.org
INTERNATIONAL UNION (IUF)
www.iuf.org/www/en
Food Sovereignty
Nyeleni Synthesis Report. 2007 March.
Tansey G and Rajotte T, editors. The future control of food. London & Sterling, Virginia: Earthscan; 2008.
Street Food
www.streetfood.org

PART 5: Data Tables
AGRICULTURE
All data from FAO via various websites (see sources above).
CONSUMPTION
8 Population. Total: The state of the world's children 2007. New York: UNICEF; 2006. Rate of increase: World Health Organization. WHOSIS.
9 Water. Availability: FAO data. Access: UNDP. Human Development Report 2007. New York: UNDP, 2007.
10 Calories FAO. **11 Undernourished** UNDP Human Development Report 2006. **12 Meat** Consumption: FAO. Animal feed: USDA. **13 Overnourished** Animal products and sugars: FAO. CHD death rate: WHO Global Disease Burden Table 3.

Photo credits
14 © UNICEF / Ami Vitale; 16 Base map from Mountain High Maps ® © Digital Wisdom Inc; bottom: © Janis Litavnieks / iStockphoto; 18 © WFP / Ximena Loza; 19 © WFP / Clive Shirley; WFP / Paul Cadenhead ; 20 © Dzianis Miraniuk / iStockphoto; 22 © World Health Organization / Pan American Health Organization; 32 © Bas Slabbers Multimedia / iStockphoto; 36 © Compassion in World Farming; 39 © RTimages / iStockphoto; 42 © FAO / U Keren; 43 © archives / iStockphoto; 46 © Lora Santiago and Chamacos, University of California, Berkeley; 49 © Vera Bogaerts / iStockphoto; 51 © Curt Carnemark / World Bank; 52 Brazil left: © Luciney Martins, right: © Bia Pasqualino Movimento dos Trabalhadores Rurais Sem Terra; India © Janadesh 2007; 54 © FAO; 55 top: © Jannet King, bottom: © Axel Drescher; 64 © World Bank / Edwin Huffman; 78 © Slobo Mitic / iStockphoto; 80 © FAO / P Cenini; 84 © Vladimir Jovanovic / iStockphoto; 91 © Christine Glade / iStockphoto, © Rafa Irusta / iStockphoto; 96 © Isabelle Lewis; 101 top: © Candida Lacey; bottom: © Joel Catchlove from set available on flikr; 102 © Juergen Sack / iStockphoto.

Index